編者的話

親愛的讀者:

今天,我的好朋友,兩岸達人,鍾藏政董事長,傳來好消息,我在「抖音」的粉絲,已經超過10萬人,並且在急速成長中。我是一個很會把握機會的人,一個月前,北京「101名師工廠」董事長Alex邀請我時,立即無條件答應,**能夠一次上課有百萬人聽到,能夠把自己的「好方法」和人分享,是人生最大的幸福!**

看了梵谷的傳記,他一生窮困潦倒,生前的畫打破傳統,被排斥,他氣得把畫當柴火燒,死後100多年,竟然被別人標售「向日葵」一億美金。所以,我從來沒有預期,在我有生之年,我這種「革命性」的發明,會被大家接受。

我的方法:學習外語,應該先從「說」開始。音標、字母,都先不要學,而且要學就學「有教養的英語」,一次背三個「極短的句子」,並且要「馬上能夠用得到」。例如:Thank you. I appreciate it. You're very kind. 這三句話,不是天天都可以用得到嗎?學了要馬上能夠使用,才有成就感,要使用,才不會忘記,只有不忘記,才能累積,否則背到後面,忘記前面,太划不來了!背一句會忘記,三個句子一起,說起來熱情,又不容易忘記。

「啞巴英語」危害人類兩百多年,大家浪費時間,就是浪費生命,苦學英文的人,方法不對,到最後大都「絕望」收尾,吃虧太大了!

每天說三句，英文不進步都難

昨天，和美國老師Edward逛街，他說：I know this place. I've been here before. 我們想不出第三句，沒有想到，小芝突然冒出一句：I remember now. 這三句話合在一起，說出來多棒。

晚上，我們在「康迎鼎」用餐，巧遇Vie Show老闆翁明顯一家人在自家用餐，又造了三句優美的英文：This place is excellent. I highly recommend it. I give it two thumbs up. 我們把restaurant說成place，這三句話便可天天使用了。

發音是原罪，經過苦練的英文最美

我有一位朋友，台灣大學外文系畢業，當了助教，最後升到教授退休，他是好學生、好老師，一路上走來都是名人。他寫了一封英文信給我，看起來很棒，但是，給美國老師一看，錯誤百出，慘不忍睹。這是傳統英語學習的典型結果，也就是說，用傳統方法，自行造句，到美國留學，和美國人結婚，無論多麼努力，英文永遠沒有學好的一天。

我發明的方法：背「現成的句子」，以三句為一組，先學會說，不要管發音，很多英文老師喜歡糾正發音，反而害了小孩，讓他們失去信心，終生不敢說英文。我強烈建議英文老師：Encourage students. Don't discourage them. Don't correct pronunciation. 發音是「原罪」，有我們中國口音，經過苦練的英文最美。The most beautiful English comes from hard work. 我的英文都是「背」的，我說出來自然有信心。

有人問我文法要不要學？當然要，美國人寫的文法書，很膚淺，把美國人害死了，很多美國人，不敢寫文章。我們國、高中文法書，還使用清朝的文法術語，文言文，把學生害死了！基本文法，一定要學，只要會做「極簡高中文法1000題」，便知道句子正確與否。需要這些資料，可以找長沙新航綫黃芬老師。現在，大家只要看「快手」和「抖音」我發表的免費「作品」即可。

「進步」讓我每天快樂！

　　我的同學告訴我：「你已經75歲，一隻腳已經踏進墳墓，不要再工作了！」其實，我從來沒有感覺自己是個老人，我覺得我還是「小孩」，每天在成長，**「進步」讓我每天快樂**。

　　很多人在網路上說：「我們是中國人，為什麼要學英文？」這是心理學上的酸葡萄作用，非常正常。傳統學「國際音標」、「漢語拼音」，文言文的文法術語像「賓語」、「狀語」，害大家失去學英文的信心。美國小孩是會說話後，才學閱讀和語法、背單字。學習是件快快樂樂的事，你試試看，不要拿課本，直接和外國老師聊天，你就在進步！

　　我不願意回到30歲，因為那時沒錢，什麼也不懂，一位大陸朋友都沒有；不願回到上個月，因為我還沒有在「快手」教英文。現在，通訊進步太快，手機是最好的老師，裡面有無數人的智慧。我希望能夠在短時間內，讓大家學會英文。「**擊敗啞巴英語**」是我一生的心願！

劉毅

TEST 1 詳解

聽力：是非題

Taipei

1. (**N**) It is raining in Taipei.
   台北正在下雨。
   * rain〔ren〕*v.* 下雨

2. (**Y**) The girl is ice-skating.
   女孩在溜冰。
   * ice-skate〔'aɪs‚sket〕*v.* 溜冰

3. (**N**) There are five apples on the table.

桌上有五顆蘋果。

* ***there + be*** 有～　　apple〔'æpl̩〕*n.* 蘋果

table〔'tebl̩〕*n.* 桌子

4. (**N**) The girl is 12 years old.

女孩今年 12 歲。

* *~years old* ～歲

5. (**Y**) The man is wearing glasses.

男士戴著眼鏡。

　　* wear〔wɛr〕v. 穿；戴　　glasses〔'glæsɪz〕n. pl. 眼鏡

6. (**Y**) The taxi driver is wearing his seat belt.

計程車司機繫著安全帶。

　　* taxi〔'tæksɪ〕n. 計程車　　driver〔'draɪvɚ〕n. 司機
　　　wear〔wɛr〕v. 配戴著　　*seat belt* 安全帶

7. (**Y**) The girl is wearing a skirt.

女孩穿著裙子。

* wear〔wɛr〕v. 穿著   skirt〔skɜt〕n. 裙子

8. (**N**) The boy is sitting on the floor.

男孩坐在地板上。

* sit〔sɪt〕v. 坐   floor〔flor〕n. 地板

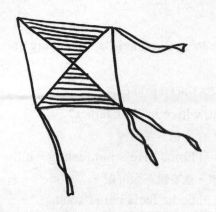

9. (**Y**) This is a kite.

這是一支風箏。

* kite〔kaɪt〕*n.* 風箏

10. (**N**) This is a basketball.

這是一顆籃球。

* basketball〔'bæskɪt,bɔl〕*n.* 籃球

聽力：選擇題

11. (**B**) Question : Why did David's father stay at home?

問：爲什麼大衛的爸爸待在家？

W：David, where is your father?

女：大衛，你的爸爸在哪裡？

M：He is at home.　He's not feeling well.

男：他在家。他身體不太舒服。

W：Oh, I hope he feels better soon.

女：喔，我希望他很快就復原。

M：Thanks.

男：謝謝。

　A. He missed the train.　他錯過火車。
　B. He is not feeling well.　<u>他身體不太舒服。</u>
　C. No, he's not home.　不，他不在家。

* stay〔ste〕*v.* 停留　　well〔wɛl〕*adj.* 健康的
　hope〔hop〕*v.* 希望　　soon〔sun〕*adv.* 很快
　miss〔mɪs〕*v.* 錯過　　train〔tren〕*n.* 火車

12. (**A**) Question: Why do the speakers like their teacher?

問：說話者爲何喜歡他們的老師？

W：Ms. Jones is my favorite teacher.

女：瓊斯女士是我最喜歡的老師。

M：Mine, too.　She's very patient and kind.

男：也是我最喜歡的。她很有耐心而且親切。

W：I enjoy being in her class.　.

女：我喜歡上她的課。

M：Me, too.

男：我也是。

A. She is patient and kind. 她很有耐心而且親切。

B. They don't like her. 他們不喜歡她。

C. Yes, they like her. 是的，他們喜歡她。

* like〔laɪk〕*v.* 喜歡　　Ms.〔mɪz〕*n.* 女士

Jones〔dʒonz〕*n.* 瓊斯　　favorite〔'fevərɪt〕*adj.* 最喜愛的

teacher〔'titʃə〕*n.* 老師

mine〔maɪn〕*pron.* 我的東西【在此指 my favorite teacher】

patient〔'peʃənt〕*adj.* 有耐心的　　kind〔kaɪnd〕*adj.* 親切的

enjoy〔ɪn'dʒɔɪ〕*v.* 喜歡；享受　　class〔klæs〕*n.* 班級；課堂

13. (**A**) Question： How often does the woman use her computer?

問：女士多常使用電腦？

M： Do you have a computer at home?

男：妳家裡有電腦嗎？

W： I do, but I seldom use it.

女：我有，但是很少用。

M： Why is that?

男：為什麼？

W： I'm too busy, so I seldom have free time.

女：我太忙了，很少有空閒時間。

A. Seldom. 不常。

B. Every day. 每天。

C. Often. 常常。

* *how often* 多常；多久一次　　often〔'ɔfən〕*adv.* 常常

computer〔kəm'pjutə〕*n.* 電腦　　seldom〔'sɛldəm〕*adv.* 很少

use〔juz〕*v.* 使用　　busy〔'bɪzɪ〕*adj.* 忙碌的

14. (**A**) Question：Where are the speakers?

問：說話者在哪裡？

W： The cafeteria is crowded today.

女：自助餐廳今天很擁擠。

M：Yes. Many people like to eat lunch here.

男：是的。很多人喜歡在這裡吃午餐。

W：Where should we sit?

女：我們應該坐在哪裡？

M：Let's sit by the window.

男：我們坐在窗邊吧。

A. In a cafeteria. 在自助餐廳。

B. In a theater. 在電影院。

C. In a library. 在圖書館。

* cafeteria〔͵kæfə'tırıə〕n. 自助餐廳
  crowded〔'kraʊdıd〕adj. 擁擠的　　lunch〔lʌntʃ〕n. 午餐
  sit〔sıt〕v. 坐　　by〔baı〕prep. 在…旁邊
  window〔'wındo〕n. 窗戶　　theater〔'θıətə〕n. 電影院
  library〔'laı͵brɛrı〕n. 圖書館

15.（ **B** ） Question：What does the girl want to do?

問：女孩想要做什麼？

M：Mary, go to bed now.

男：瑪麗，現在去睡覺。

W：Oh, Dad! I want to watch this movie.

女：喔，爸爸！我想要看這部電影。

M：How much longer until the end?

男：還要多久才結束？

W：Maybe 15 minutes.

女：可能十五分鐘。

A. Go to sleep. 去睡覺。

B. Watch a movie. 看電影。

C. Finish her homework. 做完功課。

* **go to bed** 去睡覺　　oh〔o〕*interj.* 喔
watch〔watʃ〕*v.* 看；觀賞　　movie〔'muvɪ〕*n.* 電影
how much longer 還要多久　　until〔ən'tɪl〕*prep.* 直到
end〔ɛnd〕*n.* 結束　　maybe〔'mebɪ〕*adv.* 或許；可能
minute〔'mɪnɪt〕*n.* 分鐘　　**go to sleep** 去睡覺
finish〔'fɪnɪʃ〕*v.* 做完

16. (**C**) Question : What will the man do this weekend?

問：男士這個週末要做什麼？

W : We are going to the beach on Sunday. Do you want to
　　 come with us?

女：我們星期天要去海邊。你要和我們一起去嗎？

M : I'm sorry. I can't.

男：很抱歉。我不能去。

W : What will you do this weekend?

女：你這個週末要做什麼？

M : I have to study. I have a big exam on Monday.

男：我必須讀書。我星期一有一個重要的考試。

W : Oh, that's too bad.

女：喔，真遺憾。

A. Take an exam. 參加考試。
B. Go to the beach. 去海邊。
C. Study for an exam. 讀書準備考試。

* weekend〔'wik'ɛnd〕*n.* 週末　　beach〔bitʃ〕*n.* 海邊
study〔'stʌdɪ〕*v.* 讀書　　big〔bɪg〕*adj.* 大的；重要的
exam〔ɪg'zæm〕*n.* 考試　　Monday〔'mʌnde〕*n.* 星期一
take an exam 參加考試

17. (**C**) Question : What is the woman doing?

問：女士正在做什麼？

M : What are you writing, Susan?

男：妳在寫什麼，蘇珊？

W : I'm writing a love letter to my boyfriend. He is in Canada.

女：我正在寫情書給我的男朋友。他在加拿大。

M : Oh, what is he doing in Canada?

男：喔，他在加拿大做什麼？

W : He's studying English there.

女：他在那裏學英文。

A. Looking for a boyfriend. 尋找男朋友。

B. Going overseas. 出國。

C. Writing a letter. 寫信。

* write〔raɪt〕v. 寫　　　Susan〔'susən〕n. 蘇珊
   love letter 情書　　boyfriend〔'bɔɪ͵frɛnd〕n. 男朋友
   Canada〔'kænədə〕n. 加拿大
   study〔'stʌdɪ〕v. 研讀　　*look for* 尋找
   overseas〔'ovɚ'siz〕adv. 在國外；到國外
   go overseas 出國　　letter〔'lɛtɚ〕n. 信

18. (**A**) Question : Where are they?

問：他們在哪裡？

W : This is a great place to eat breakfast. Have you seen the
    menu?

女：在這個地方吃早餐很棒。你已經看了菜單嗎？

M : Yeah. What do you usually order?

男：是的。妳通常會點什麼？

W : I always order the country breakfast. It's three pancakes,
    four eggs, bacon, sausage, toast, and a cup of fruit.

女：我總是點鄉村早餐。有三片薄煎餅、四個蛋、培根、香腸、吐
    司，和一杯水果。

M : Wow, that's a lot of food!

男：哇，好多食物！

A. In a restaurant. 在餐廳裡。

B. In the country. 在鄉下。

C. In the kitchen. 在廚房。

* great〔glæd〕*adj.* 高興的　　place〔ples〕*n.* 地點；場所
  breakfast〔'brɛkfəst〕*n.* 早餐　　menu〔'mɛnju〕*n.* 菜單
  yeah〔jæ〕*adv.* 是的（= *yes*）　　usually〔'juʒʊəlɪ〕*adv.* 通常
  order〔'ɔrdɚ〕*v.* 點（菜）
  country〔'kʌntrɪ〕*adj.* 鄉村的　*n.* 鄉村；鄉下；國家
  pancake〔'pæn,kek〕*n.* 薄煎餅　　egg〔ɛg〕*n.* 蛋；雞蛋
  bacon〔'bekən〕*n.* 培根　　sausage〔'sɔsɪdʒ〕*n.* 香腸
  toast〔tost〕*n.* 土司　　fruit〔frut〕*n.* 水果
  wow〔waʊ〕*interj.*（表示驚訝、喜悅等）哇　*a lot of* 很多
  food〔fud〕*n.* 食物　　restaurant〔'rɛstərənt〕*n.* 餐廳
  kitchen〔'kɪtʃɪn〕*n.* 廚房

19. (**C**) Question : Where is the man going?

    問：男士要去哪裡？

    M : I'm going to the cleaners.　Do you need anything while I'm out?

    男：我要去洗衣店。我外出時妳有需要任何東西嗎？

    W : Yes. Would you go to the post office and send a package for me?　Here it is.

    女：有，你可以順路去郵局幫我寄包裹嗎？拿去吧。

    M : No problem.　Anything else?

    男：沒問題。還有其他的事嗎？

    W : No, thank you.

    女：沒了，謝謝。

    A. To his office. 到他的辦公室。

    B. To the hospital and the supermarket. 去醫院和超市。

C. To the cleaners and the post office. 去洗衣店和郵局。

* cleaner (ˈklinɚ) *n.* 清潔工；洗衣店的老闆
  the cleaners 洗衣店　　out (aut) *adv.* 外出
  stop by 中途順便到　　***post office*** 郵局
  send (sɛnd) *v.* 寄　　package (ˈpækɪdʒ) *n.* 包裹
  Here it is. 你要的東西在這裡；拿去吧。
  problem (ˈprɑbləm) *n.* 問題　　else (ɛls) *adj.* 其他的；別的
  office (ˈɔfɪs) *n.* 辦公室　　hospital (ˈhɑspɪtl̩) *n.* 醫院
  supermarket (ˈsupɚˌmɑrkɪt) *n.* 超級市場

20. (**B**) Question : Why doesn't the man eat the pizza?

問：為什麼男士不吃披薩？

W : This pizza is delicious. Do you want some?

女：這披薩真好吃。你想要一些嗎？

M : No, it looks great, but I'm on a diet.

男：不，看起來很棒，但是我在節食。

W : Yes, I noticed that you have gained weight.

女：是的，我注意到你變胖了。

M : I have, but I'm going to lose five kilograms.

男：我是變胖了，但我要減五公斤。

A. He has to go to work. 他必須去上班。

B. He is on a diet. 他在節食。

C. He doesn't like pizza. 他不喜歡披薩。

* pizza (ˈpitsə) *n.* 披薩　　delicious (dɪˈliʃəs) *adj.* 好吃的
  look (luk) *adj.* 看起來　　great (gret) *adj.* 很棒的
  on a diet 節食　　notice (ˈnotɪs) *v.* 注意到
  gain (gen) *v.* 增加　　weight (wet) *n.* 重量；體重
  gain weight 體重增加；變胖　　***be going to*** 將要
  lose (luz) *v.* 減輕　　kilogram (ˈkɪləˌgræm) *n.* 公斤
  go to work 去上班

TEST 2 詳解

聽力：是非題

1. (**Y**) Jack is sitting on a chair.

　　 傑克正坐在椅子上。

　　 * sit〔sɪt〕v. 坐　　chair〔tʃɛr〕n. 椅子

2. (**Y**) Lucy is wearing a hat and a tie.

　　 露西戴著一頂帽子，並打了一條領帶。

　　 * wear〔wɛr〕v. 穿；戴　　hat〔hæt〕n. 帽子
　　　 tie〔taɪ〕n. 領帶

3. (**N**) This is a television.

這是一台電視。

　* television (ˈtɛləˌvɪʒən) *n.* 電視

4. (**N**) Steve is writing a story.

史蒂夫正在寫一個故事。

　* write (raɪt) *v.* 寫　　story (ˈstɔrɪ) *n.* 故事

5. (**Y**)　They are riding a train.

　　　　　他們正搭乘火車。

　　　　　* ride〔raɪd〕*v.* 騎；搭乘　　　train〔tren〕*n.* 火車

6. (**Y**)　Mrs. Jackson is a teacher.

　　　　　傑克遜太太是老師。

　　　　　* Mrs.〔'mɪsɪz〕*n.* 太太　　　teacher〔'titʃɚ〕*n.* 老師

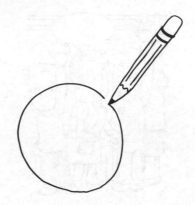

7. (**Y**) Tom drew a circle with a pencil.

湯姆用鉛筆畫了一個圓。

* drew〔dru〕v. 畫【draw 的過去式】　　circle〔'sɜkḷ〕n. 圓
　　pencil〔'pɛnsḷ〕n. 鉛筆

8. (**N**) He is a bank manager.

他是一位銀行經理。

* bank〔bæŋk〕n. 銀行　　manager〔'mænɪdʒɚ〕n. 經理

9. (**Y**) He is listenIng to music.

他正在聽音樂。

* *listen to* 聽　　music ('mjuzɪk) n. 音樂

10. (**N**) Frank put the book in his desk.

法蘭克把書放在他的書桌上。

* desk (dɛsk) n. 書桌

聽力：選擇題

11. (**A**) Question : What are they talking about?

問：他們正在談論什麼？

W : That's a nice watch, John. Where did you get it?

女：那是一只很好的手錶，約翰。你在哪裡買的？

M : My mother gave it to me. I think she bought it at a department store.

男：我媽媽給我的。我想她是在百貨公司買的。

W : It looks expensive.

女：它看起來很貴。

M : I don't know how much it cost.

男：我不知道多少錢。

A. The man's watch. 男士的手錶。

B. The woman's mother. 女士的媽媽。

C. The department store. 百貨公司。

* ***talk about*** 談論　　nice〔naɪs〕*adj.* 好的；漂亮的
watch〔watʃ〕*n.* 手錶　　get〔gɛt〕*v.* 獲得；買
bought〔bɔt〕*v.* 買【buy 的過去式】　　***department store*** 百貨公司
look〔luk〕*v.* 看起來　　expensive〔ɪk'spɛnsɪv〕*adj.* 昂貴的
cost〔kɔst〕*v.* 值（多少錢）

12. (**C**) Question : Did Cindy have a good day?

問：辛蒂今天過得愉快嗎？

M : Did you have a good day at school, Cindy?

男：妳今天在學校過得好嗎，辛蒂？

W : No, it was very bad. I failed my English quiz and I forgot to finish my math homework.

女：不好，很糟糕。我英文小考不及格，而且我忘了做完我的數學作業。

M : That's too bad. Are your parents angry?

男：真糟糕。妳的父母很生氣嗎？

W : No, but they want me to work harder.

女：沒有，我不過他們要我再用功一點。

A. Yes, she feels great. 是的，她覺得很棒。

B. It was Monday. 是星期一。

C. No. She had a bad day. 不，她今天不順利。

* ***have a good day*** 有愉快的一天
  fail〔fel〕*v.* (考試) 不及格　　quiz〔kwɪz〕*n.* 小考
  forgot〔fɚˈgɑt〕*v.* 忘記【forget 的過去式】
  finish〔ˈfɪnɪʃ〕*v.* 完成　　math〔mæθ〕*n.* 數學
  homework〔ˈhomˌwɝk〕*n.* 功課
  That's too bad. 眞糟糕。　　parents〔ˈpɛrənts〕*n. pl.* 父母
  angry〔ˈæŋgrɪ〕*adj.* 生氣的　　take〔tek〕*v.* 參加 (考試)
  work hard 努力；用功　　great〔gret〕*adj.* 很棒的
  have a bad day 過得不順利；諸事不順

13. (**C**) Question : Where are they?

問：他們在哪裡？

W : Are you ready to order?

女：您準備好點餐了嗎？

M : Yes, I'll have the chicken sandwich and a Coke.

男：是的，我要雞肉三明治和一杯可口可樂。

W : Would you like French fries or potato chips with the sandwich?

女：您想要薯條還是洋芋片搭配三明治呢？

M : Can I have both? I'm pretty hungry.

男：我可以兩個都要嗎？我好餓。

A. In a library. 在圖書館裡。

B. In a train station. 在火車站。

C. In a restaurant. 在餐廳。

* ready〔ˈrɛdɪ〕*adj.* 準備好的　　order〔ˈɔrdɚ〕*v.* 點菜
  chicken〔ˈtʃɪkɪn〕*n.* 雞肉　　sandwich〔ˈsændwɪtʃ〕*n.* 三明治
  Coke〔kok〕*n.* 可口可樂 (= *Coca-Cola*)

> *would like* 想要　　*French fries* 薯條
> *potato chips* 洋芋片　　pretty (ˈprɪtɪ) *adv.* 非常
> hungry (ˈhʌŋgrɪ) *adj.* 飢餓的
> library (ˈlaɪˌbrɛrɪ) *n.* 圖書館　　*train station* 火車站
> restaurant (ˈrɛstərənt) *n.* 餐廳

14. (**A**) Question : Did the girl win a race?

　　問：女孩贏得賽跑了嗎？

　　M : How did you do in the race, Helen?

　　男：妳賽跑表現如何呀，海倫？

　　W : Pretty good. I came in second in the 100-meter race.

　　女：很好。我 100 公尺賽跑第二名。

　　M : Wow, that's great! You must be proud of yourself.

　　男：哇，那很棒！妳一定以妳自己為榮。

　　W : I guess so. Maybe I will win next time.

　　女：我想是吧。或許我下一次能贏。

　　A. No, she didn't. <u>不，她沒有。</u>

　　B. Yes. She won the 100-meter race.

　　　　是的。她 100 公尺賽跑贏了。

　　C. She didn't run in the race. 她沒去參加賽跑。

　　* win (wɪn) *v.* 贏　　race (res) *n.* 賽跑　　do (du) *v.* 表現
　　come in second 得第二名　　meter (ˈmitɚ) *n.* 公尺
　　wow (waʊ) *interj.* （表示驚訝、喜悅等）哇
　　great (gret) *adj.* 很棒的
　　proud (praʊd) *adj.* 驕傲的；感到光榮的
　　be proud of 以…為榮　　guess (gɛs) *v.* 猜；想；認為
　　maybe (ˈmebi) *adv.* 或許；可能
　　next time 下一次　　run (rʌn) *v.* 跑

15. (**C**) Question : Will the man have an exam tomorrow?

　　問：男士明天會有考試嗎？

　　W : So that is the end of today's class. Does anyone have
　　　　any questions? Yes, Bill?

女：那今天的講課就到此結束。有人有任何問題嗎？什麼事，比爾？

M : Will this be on tomorrow's exam?

男：這會出現在明天的考試嗎？

W : Yes. You should review everything you learned today.

女：會的。但是你應該要複習今天學的。

M : Okay.

男：好的。

A. No. He doesn't have any questions.

　　沒有。他沒有任何問題。

B. No, he doesn't want to have an exam.

　　沒有。他不想要有任何考試。

C. Yes, he will have an exam. 有，他會有考試。

* exam〔ɪgˊzæm〕*n.* 考試　　so〔so〕*adv.* 那樣；這樣
  end〔ɛnd〕*n.* 結束　　class〔klæs〕*n.* 講課
  question〔ˊkwɛstʃən〕*n.* 問題
  yes〔jɛs〕*adv.* (回答呼喚) 什麼事？　　review〔rɪˊvju〕*v.* 複習
  okay〔ˊoˊke〕*adv.* 好的 (= O.K.)

16. (**C**) Question : What did the woman buy at the department store?

　　問：那女士在百貨公司買了什麼？

M : How was your trip to the department store, Kelly? Did you buy anything?

男：妳去了百貨公司一趟，如何呀，凱莉？妳有買任何東西嗎？

W : No, I didn't see anything I wanted. So I didn't buy anything.

女：沒有，我沒有看到任何我想要的。所以我什麼都沒買。

M : That's OK. You also didn't spend any money.

男：沒關係。妳也沒花到錢。

W : But I really need to find a new dress for the party this weekend.

女：但我真的想要找一件洋裝，穿去這週末的派對。

A. A new dress. 一件新的洋裝。

B. Everything she wanted. 她想要的所有東西。

C. Nothing. <u>什麼也沒買。</u>

* trip〔trɪp〕*n.* 旅行；走一趟　　want〔wɑnt〕*v.* 想要
That's OK. 沒關係。　　spend〔spɛnd〕*v.* 花費
dress〔drɛs〕*n.* 洋裝　　party〔'pɑrtɪ〕*n.* 派對
weekend〔'wik'ɛnd〕*n.* 週末
nothing〔'nʌθɪŋ〕*pron.* （什麼也）沒有

17. (**B**) Question : Can the man speak French?

問：男士會說法文嗎？

W : Is this your first time in France?

女：這是你第一次來法國嗎？

M : No, I've been here many times. My grandfather lives here. We visit him every summer.

男：不是，我已經來這裡很多次了。我爺爺住在這裡。我們每年夏天都會來拜訪他。

W : Wow, that's really great! Do you speak French?

女：哇，那真是太棒了！你會說法文嗎？

M : Yes, I speak some French.

男：是的，我會講一些法文。

A. He lives in France. 他住在法國。

B. Yes, he can speak some French. <u>是的，他會說一些法文。</u>

C. No. He has never been to France. 不，他從未去過法國。

* French〔frɛntʃ〕*n.* 法文　　time〔taɪm〕*n.* 次數
first time 第一次　　France〔fræns〕*n.* 法國
grandfather〔'græn,fɑðə〕*n.* 祖父；爺爺
visit〔'vɪzɪt〕*v.* 拜訪
have never been to 從未去過

18. (**B**) Question : What do we know about George?

問：關於喬治，我們知道什麼？

M : Did you hear about George?

男：妳有聽說關於喬治的事嗎？

W : No, what happened to him?

女：沒有，他發生什麼事了？

M : He was fighting in school.

男：他在學校打架。

W : George?! I don't believe it. He is such a nice boy.

女：喬治？！我不相信。他是一個很好的男孩。

A. He is in the hospital. 他在醫院。

B. He was fighting at school. 他在學校打架。

C. He was the best student in class. 他是班上最棒的學生。

* ***hear about*** 聽說　　happen (ˈhæpən) *v.* 發生 < *to* >
fight (faɪt) *v.* 打架　　believe (bɪˈliv) *v.* 相信
such (sʌtʃ) *adj.* 如此；非常　　hospital (ˈhɑspɪtl̩) *n.* 醫院
in class 在班上

19. (**C**) Question : What is Alien Zombies?

問：什麼是「外星人殭屍」？

W : Did you see Alien Zombies?

女：你看過「外星人殭屍」了嗎？

M : Yes, and I can't wait to see it again.

男：有，而我等不及再看一遍。

W : Me too! I saw it at the movie theater last week, but I
want to go again.

女：我也是，我上星期去電影院看的，但是我還想再去看一遍。

M : OK. Let's go see it again tonight.

男：好的。我們今晚再去看一次吧。

A. A song. 一首歌。

B. A painting. 一幅畫。

C. A movie. 一部電影。

* alien (ˊeljən) *n.* 外星人　　zombie (ˊzɑmbɪ) *n.* 殭屍
wait (wet) *v.* 等待　***can't wait to V.*** 等不及～
again (əˊgɛn) *adv.* 再；又　　movie (ˊmuvɪ) *n.* 電影
theater (ˊθiətɚ) *n.* 電影院
go see it 去看 (= *go to see it* = *go and see it*)
song (sɔŋ) *n.* 歌曲　　painting (ˊpentɪŋ) *n.* 畫

20. (**A**) Question : What did the man do?
問：這位男士做了什麼？

M : Hello, I found a kitten in the park. I think it is lost.
男：喂，我在公園發現一隻小貓。我想牠走失了。

W : You can bring it to our animal shelter. We will keep the
kitten until we find the owner.
女：你可以把牠帶到我們的動物收容所。我們會養這隻小貓，直到
牠找到主人為止。

M: Where are you?
男：你們位於哪裡呢？

W: At the corner of Logan Boulevard and Lincoln Avenue.
女：在洛根大道和林肯大道的轉角。

A. He found a kitten. 他發現一隻小貓。

B. He bought a dog. 他買了一隻狗。

C. He made a new friend. 他交了一個新朋友。

* hello (hɛˊlo) *interj.* （打電話時）喂　　kitten (ˊkɪtn̩) *n.* 小貓
park (pɑrk) *n.* 公園　　lost (lɔst) *adj.* 迷路的；走失的
animal (ˊænəml̩) *n.* 動物　　shelter (ˊʃɛltɚ) *n.* 庇護所；收容所
keep (kip) *v.* 養；飼養　　until (ənˊtɪl) *conj.* 到…為止
owner (ˊonɚ) *n.* 擁有者；主人　　corner (ˊkɔrnɚ) *n.* 轉角
Logan (ˊlogən) *n.* 洛根　　boulevard (ˊbuləˏvɑrd) *n.* 大道
Lincoln (ˊlɪŋkən) *n.* 林肯　　avenue (ˊævəˏnju) *n.* 大道
make a friend 交了一個朋友

TEST 3 詳解

聽力：是非題

1. (**Y**) The rabbit is eating carrots.

兔子在吃紅蘿蔔。

* rabbit〔'ræbɪt〕*n.* 兔子　　carrot〔'kærət〕*n.* 紅蘿蔔

Peter

2. (**Y**) Peter is a doctor.

彼得是醫生。

* doctor〔'dɑktɚ〕*n.* 醫生

3. (**N**) He is riding a bicycle.

他在騎腳踏車。

* ride〔raɪd〕*v.* 騎　　bicycle〔'baɪ͵sɪkl̩〕*n.* 腳踏車

Mr. Martin

4. (**N**) Mr. Martin is a fireman.

馬汀先生是消防員。

* Mr.〔'mɪstɚ〕*n.* 先生　　fireman〔'faɪrmən〕*n.* 消防員

5. (**Y**) He is watching baseball on television.

他正在看電視的棒球比賽。

* baseball〔'bes,bɔl〕*n.* 棒球（比賽）
  television〔'tɛlə,vɪʒən〕*n.* 電視

6. (**N**) The boys are fighting over a book.

男孩們正在為一本書爭吵。

* fight〔faɪt〕*v.* 打架；爭吵　　over〔'ovɚ〕*prep.* 為了⋯事

7. (**N**) The woman is holding her cat.

　　　女士正抱著她的貓。

　　　* hold〔hold〕*v.* 抱著

8. (**N**) He is giving a weather report.

　　　他正在播報氣象。

　　　* give〔gɪv〕*v.* 提供　　weather〔'wɛðɚ〕*n.* 天氣；氣象
　　　report〔rɪ'port〕*n.* 報告

9. (**Y**) The man spilled wine on the table.

男士把酒灑在桌上。

* spill〔spɪl〕v. 潑；灑　　wine〔waɪn〕n. 酒
table〔'tebl〕n. 桌子

10. (**N**) This is a cat.

這是一隻貓。

* cat〔kæt〕n. 貓

聽力：選擇題

11. (**C**) Question : Who is the woman?

問：這位女士是誰？

W : Welcome back, Jason. Here's your mail.

女：歡迎回來，傑森。這是你的信。

M : Thank you for collecting it. You're a good neighbor.

男：謝謝妳幫我拿信。妳是個好鄰居。

W : How was your vacation?

女：你的假期如何？

M : It was very nice.

男：很好。

A. The man's mail carrier. 男士的郵差。

B. The man's wife. 男士的妻子。

C. The man's neighbor. <u>男士的鄰居。</u>

* mail〔mel〕 *n.* 信件　　collect〔kəˈlɛkt〕 *v.* 收集；拿回
  neighbor〔ˈnebɚ〕 *n.* 鄰居　　vacation〔veˈkeʃən〕 *n.* 假期
  carrier〔ˈkærɪɚ〕 *n.* 運送人；信差　　***mail carrier*** 郵差
  wife〔waɪf〕 *n.* 妻子

12. (**A**) Question : What did the woman buy?

問：女士買了什麼？

W : How much do these shirts cost?

女：這些襯衫要多少錢？

M : They are 200 dollars each.

男：每一件兩百美元。

W : I'll take one—a red one, please.

女：我要買一件——請給我紅色的。

M : Here you are.

男：拿去吧。

A. A red shirt. 一件紅色的襯衫。

B. 200 shirts. 兩百件襯衫。

C. Nothing. 什麼都沒買。

* shirt〔ʃɝt〕*n.* 襯衫　　cost〔kɔst〕*v.* 值（多少錢）
each〔itʃ〕*adv.* 每件　　nothing〔ˋnʌθɪŋ〕*pron.*（什麼也）沒有

13. (**B**) Question : Where are they?

問：他們在哪裡？

M : Ms. Yang! What a pleasant surprise. What are you
doing here?

男：楊女士！真是令人愉快的驚喜。妳在這裡做什麼？

W : Hello, Tom. I'm having some ice cream. How about
you?

女：哈囉，湯姆。我正在吃冰淇淋。你呢？

M : I'm going to have some ice cream, too. I've never seen
you at this shop before. Do you come here often?

男：我也正要吃些冰淇淋。我以前從來沒有在這家店看過妳。
妳常來這裡嗎？

W : Not really.

女：並沒有。

A. In a classroom. 在教室裡。

B. In an ice cream shop. 在一家冰淇淋店。

C. In the woman's home. 在女士的家裡。

* Ms.〔mɪz〕*n.* 女士　　pleasant〔ˋplɛzn̩t〕*adj.* 令人愉快的
surprise〔səˋpraɪz〕*n.* 驚訝的事；意外的事
hello〔həˋlo〕*interj.*（用於打招呼）哈囉
have〔hæv〕*v.* 吃　　ice cream〔ˋaɪsˏkrim〕*n.* 冰淇淋
How about you? 你呢？　　shop〔ʃɑp〕*n.* 商店
before〔bɪˋfor〕*adv.* 以前　　often〔ˋɔfən〕*adv.* 常常
not really 不完全是　　classroom〔ˋklæsˏrum〕*n.* 教室

14. (**A**) Question : How does Joe look?

問：喬看起來如何？

W : Joe is so handsome, isn't he?

女：喬很英俊，不是嗎？

M : Really?　I don't think he is special.

男：眞的嗎？我不覺得他很特別。

W : Why not?　He's so tall, and he looks like a movie star.

女：爲什麼不會？他很高，而且他看起來像個電影明星。

M : Oh, so that's why all the girls like him.

男：哦，所以那就是爲何所有的女孩都喜歡他。

A. Tall and handsome.　又高又帥。

B. Not special at all.　一點也不特別。

C. Like a girl.　像個女孩。

* Joe〔dʒo〕*n.* 喬　　look〔lʊk〕*v.* 看起來
handsome〔ˈhænsəm〕*adj.* 英俊的
really〔ˈrɪəlɪ〕*adv.*（表示輕微的驚訝、懷疑）咦；眞的
special〔ˈspɛʃəl〕*adj.* 特別的　　***Why not?*** 爲什麼不？
tall〔tɔl〕*adj.* 高的　　star〔stɑr〕*n.* 明星
oh〔o〕*interj.*（引出答話或評論）哦　　girl〔gɝl〕*n.* 女孩
like〔laɪk〕*prep.* 像　*v.* 喜歡　　***not…at all*** 一點也不…

15. (**B**) Question : When should you eat cherries?

問：你應該何時吃櫻桃？

M : When is the best time to eat cherries?

男：什麼時候吃櫻桃最好？

W : In the summer.　That's when they are in season.

女：夏季。夏季是它們的盛產期。

M : Do you know what fruit is good now?

男：你知道什麼水果適合現在吃嗎？

W : Blueberries and green apples are good.

女：很適合吃藍莓和青蘋果。

A. Winter. 冬天。

B. Summer. <u>夏天。</u>

C. Right now. 現在。

* cherry〔ˋtʃɛrɪ〕*n.* 櫻桃　　summer〔ˋsʌmɚ〕*n.* 夏季
season〔ˋsizn̩〕*n.* 季節　　***in season*** 盛產的；當季的
fruit〔frut〕*n.* 水果　　good〔gʊd〕*adj.* 好的；有益健康的
blueberry〔ˋbluˌbɛrɪ〕*n.* 藍莓　　***green apple*** 青蘋果
winter〔ˋwɪntɚ〕*n.* 冬天　　***right now*** 現在；目前

16. (**A**) Question : What does the man do?

問：男士做了什麼事？

W：Can I borrow some money? My wallet is at home.

女：我可以跟你借點錢嗎？我把皮夾忘在家裡了。

M：How much do you need?

男：妳需要多少？

W：At least five hundred dollars, if you have it.

女：至少五百元，如果你有的話。

M：Sure. I can lend you a thousand. You can pay me back
later.

男：當然。我可以借妳一千元。妳可以之後再還我。

A. Lend money to the woman. <u>借錢給女士。</u>

B. Leave a message. 留言。

C. Go home. 回家。

* borrow〔ˋbaro〕*v.* 借（入）　　wallet〔ˋwɑlɪt〕*n.* 皮夾
at least 至少　　hundred〔ˋhʌndrəd〕*adj.* 百的
dollar〔ˋdɑlɚ〕*n.* 元　　sure〔ʃʊr〕*adv.* 當然
lend〔lɛnd〕*v.* 借（出）　　thousand〔ˋθaʊzn̩d〕*n.* 千
pay back 償還　　later〔ˋletɚ〕*adv.* 之後
message〔ˋmɛsɪdʒ〕*n.* 訊息；留言　　***leave a message*** 留言

17. (**C**) Question : How often does the man smoke?

問：男士多久抽一次煙？

W : Do you smoke?

女：你抽煙嗎？

M : Sometimes.

男：有時候。

W : You should stop. It's very bad for your health.

女：你應該戒煙。這對你的健康不很好。

M : But I only smoke now and then. That's not too bad for me.

男：但是我只有偶爾抽煙。那對我而言不算太壞。

A. Every day. 每天。

B. Never. 從不。

C. Sometimes. <u>偶爾。</u>

* ***how often*** 多常；多久一次　　smoke〔smok〕*v.* 抽煙
sometimes〔'sʌm,taɪmz〕*adv.* 有時候　　stop〔stɑp〕*v.* 停止
bad〔bæd〕*adj.* 有害的；不好的　　health〔hɛlθ〕*n.* 健康
now and then 偶爾（= *sometimes*）　　never〔'nɛvɚ〕*adv.* 從不

18. (**C**) Question : Why did the woman leave the party?

問：女士為何離開派對？

M : Why did you leave the party last night?

男：妳昨天為何離開派對？

W : I wasn't having fun, so I left.

女：我玩得不愉快，所以離開了。

M : Were you sick?

男：妳生病了嗎？

W : No, I just didn't like the party.

女：沒有，我只是不喜歡那個派對。

A. She was sick. 她生病了。

B. She wasn't invited. 她沒有被邀請。

C. She wasn't having fun. 她玩得不愉快。

* leave〔liv〕v. 離開　　party〔'partɪ〕n. 派對
  have fun 玩得愉快　　left〔lɛft〕v. 離開【leave 的過去式】
  sick〔sɪk〕adj. 生病的　　just〔dʒʌst〕adv. 只是
  invite〔ɪn'vaɪt〕v. 邀請

19. (**C**) Question：What did the woman do yesterday?
    問：女士昨天做了什麼？

    W：I quit my job yesterday.

    女：我昨天辭職了。

    M：You did? Why did you stop working there?

    男：妳辭職了？妳為何不在那裡工作呢？

    W：I wasn't happy in my job.

    女：我做這份工作並不高興。

    M：Are you looking for a new job already?

    男：妳已經在找新工作了嗎？

    A. She started a new job. 她開始新的工作。

    B. She moved to a different city. 她搬到另一個城市。

    C. She stopped working. 她辭職了。

    * quit〔kwɪt〕v. 停止；辭（職）　　job〔dʒab〕n. 工作
      stop〔stap〕v. 停止　　work〔wɝk〕v. 工作
      happy〔'hæpɪ〕adj. 高興的　　***look for*** 尋找
      already〔ɔl'rɛdɪ〕adv. 已經　　start〔start〕v. 開始
      move〔muv〕v. 搬家　　different〔'dɪfərənt〕adj. 不同的
      city〔'sɪtɪ〕n. 城市

20. (**B**) Question：What is true about both speakers?
    問：關於兩位說話者，何者為真？

M : Excuse me.　Could you tell me where the Tonghua Night
　　Market is?

男：對不起。妳可以告訴我通化夜市在哪嗎？

W : I'm sorry, but I don't know.　I'm new in town.

女：很抱歉，我不知道。我剛到這城裡。

M : Oh, you are?　Me, too!　How long have you lived here?

男：喔，妳剛來呀？我也是！妳住在這裡多久了？

W : Two weeks.　How about you?

女：兩個禮拜。你呢？

A. They are at the Tonghua Night Market.
　　他們在通化夜市。

B. Both are new in town.　兩人都是剛到城裡。

C. Both travel by boat.　兩人都搭船旅行。

* speaker〔'spikɚ〕n. 說話者
　Excuse me.（用於引起對方注意）對不起；很抱歉。
　night market 夜市　　new〔nju〕*adj.* 剛來的
　town〔taʊn〕*n.* 城鎮；市鎮　　*How long ~?* ～多久？
　How about you? 你呢？
　travel〔'trævl̩〕*v.* 旅行　　boat〔bot〕*n.* 船
　by boat 搭船

TEST 4 詳解

聽力：是非題

1. (**N**) The waitress is ready to take an order.

女服務生準備好要接受點菜了。

* waitress (ˈwetrɪs) *n.* 女服務生　　ready (ˈrɛdɪ) *adj.* 準備好的
take an order 接受點菜

2. (**N**) Miss Lai is a doctor.

賴小姐是位醫生。

* Miss (mɪs) *n.* 小姐　　doctor (ˈdɑktə) *n.* 醫生

3.(**N**) This is an apple.

這是一顆蘋果。

* apple〔ˊæpḷ〕n. 蘋果

4.(**Y**) It is 7:00 p.m.

現在是晚上七點。

* ***p.m.*** 午後；下午 (= *post meridiem*)

5. (**Y**) It is 6:30 a.m.

現在是上午六點三十分。

* ***a.m.*** 午前;上午 (*= ante meridiem*)

6. (**N**) The man is baking a cake.

男士在烤一個蛋糕。

* bake〔bek〕*v.* 烤　　cake〔kek〕*n.* 蛋糕

7. (**N**) The lawyer speaks Chinese.

　　律師說中文。

　　* lawyer (ˈlɔjɚ) *n.* 律師　　Chinese (tʃaɪˈniz) *n.* 中文

8. (**Y**) The professor is wearing glasses.

　　教授戴著眼鏡。

　　* professor (prəˈfɛsɚ) *n.* 教授　　wear (wɛr) *v.* 穿；戴
　　glasses (ˈglæsɪz) *n. pl.* 眼鏡

9. (**N**) It is 4:25.

現在是四點二十五分。

10. (**Y**) Patty is riding a bicycle.

帕蒂正在騎腳踏車

* ride 〔 raɪd 〕 v. 騎　　bicycle 〔ˈbaɪˌsɪkḷ 〕 n. 腳踏車

聽力：選擇題

11. (**B**) Question : What should the man do?

問：男士應該做什麼？

W : Your hair is too long. You should get a haircut.

女：你的頭髮太長了。你應該剪頭髮了。

M : I know. But I can't get my hair cut right now.

男：我知道。但是我現在無法去理髮。

W : What's the problem?

女：出了什麼問題？

M : My regular barber is on vacation.

男：我常找的理髮師在休假。

A. Go on vacation.　去度假。
B. Get a haircut.　理髮。
C. Wash his hair.　洗頭髮。

* hair〔hɛr〕*n.* 頭髮　　long〔lɔŋ〕*adj.* 長的
　haircut〔'hɛr͵kʌt〕*n.* 理髮；剪髮　　***get a haircut*** 理髮
　right now 現在　　problem〔'prɑbləm〕*n.* 問題
　regular〔'rɛgjələ〕*adj.* 通常的；固定的
　barber〔'bɑrbə〕*n.*（男）理髮師　　***on vacation*** 在度假；在休假
　wash〔wɑʃ〕*v.* 洗

12. (**C**) Question : When will the woman and man have a meeting?

問：女士和男士將何時開會？

W : Can we have a meeting today or tomorrow?

女：我們可以今天或明天開會嗎？

M : I'm sorry, but I'll be busy until late this afternoon.
　　How about tomorrow morning?

男：很抱歉，我今天下午會一直忙到很晚。明天早上如何？

W : That's fine.

女：沒問題。

M : OK. I'll see you at 9:00 tomorrow.

男：好的。我們明天早上九點見。

A. This afternoon. 今天下午。

B. They won't have a meeting. 他們不會開會。

C. Tomorrow morning. 明天早上。

* meeting (ˈmitɪŋ) *n.* 會議　***haev a meeting*** 開會
busy (ˈbɪzɪ) *adj.* 忙碌的　　until (ənˈtɪl) *prep.* 直到
late (let) *adv.* 遲；晚　　***How about…?*** …如何？
That's fine. 很好；沒問題。

13. (**B**) Question : What did the boy do yesterday?

問：男孩昨天做了什麼？

M : Hi, Ms. Brown.

男：嗨，布朗女士。

W : Hello, John. What's happened?

女：哈囉，約翰。發生什麼事？

M : I'm here to say I'm sorry. I threw a ball and broke your
window yesterday. I want to pay for a new window.

男：我是來道歉的。我昨天丟球打破了妳的窗戶。我想要支付新
窗戶的費用。

W : I've already got a new window, so you don't have to pay.
Everyone makes mistakes. Saying sorry is enough.

女：我已經換好新的窗戶了，所以你不需要付錢。每個人都會犯
錯。說抱歉就足夠了。

A. He gave the woman some money. 他給了女士一些錢。

B. He broke the woman's window. 他打破女士的窗戶。

C. He won a baseball game. 他贏得一場棒球比賽。

* happen (ˈhæpən) *v.* 發生　　threw (θru) *v.* 丟【throw 的過去式】
broke (brok) *v.* 打破【break 的過去式】
window (ˈwɪndo) *n.* 窗戶
pay for 支付…的錢　　already (ɔlˈrɛdɪ) *adv.* 已經

have to V. 必須～　　mistake〔məˋstek〕*n.* 錯誤
make a mistake 犯錯　　enough〔ɪˋnʌf〕*adj.* 足夠的
gave〔gev〕*v.* 給【give 的過去式】
won〔wʌn〕*v.* 贏【win 的過去式】
baseball〔ˋbesˏbɔl〕*n.* 棒球　　game〔gem〕*n.* 比賽

14. (**A**) Question : What is the woman holding?

問：女士正在握著什麼？

W : Be careful, Jack.　Don't fall.

女：小心，傑克。別跌下來。

M : I'm fine, Mary.　Just keep holding the ladder.

男：我很好，瑪麗。只要繼續握著梯子就好。

W : My arms are tired.

女：我的手臂累了。

M : Two more minutes, OK?　Just hold the ladder.　I'm almost done.

男：再兩分鐘，可以嗎？只要握住梯子。我快要好了。

A. A ladder.　梯子。

B. Her arms.　她的手臂。

C. A clock.　一個時鐘。

* hold〔hold〕*v.* 握著　　careful〔ˋkɛrfəl〕*adj.* 小心的
fall〔fɔl〕*v.* 落下；跌落　　keep〔kip〕*v.* 持續
ladder〔ˋlædɚ〕*n.* 梯子　　arm〔arm〕*n.* 手臂
tired〔taɪrd〕*adj.* 疲倦的；累的　　minute〔ˋmɪnɪt〕*n.* 分鐘
two more minutes 再兩分鐘　　almost〔ˋɔlˏmost〕*adv.* 幾乎
done〔dʌn〕*adj.* 完成的；結束的　　clock〔klɑk〕*n.* 時鐘

15. (**C**) Question : What are the speakers doing?

問：說話者在做什麼？

M : According to the map, this road doesn't go to the city.

男：根據這張地圖，這條路沒有通往那個城市。

W : Are we going the wrong way?

女：所以我們走錯路了嗎？

M : I think so. Stop at that gas station, and I'll ask for
directions.

男：我想是的。如果在加油站停車，然後我就去問路。

W : OK. I hope someone there can help.

女：好的。我希望那裡有人可以幫忙。

A. Riding a bus. 搭乘公車。

B. Flying a plane. 開飛機。

C. Driving a car. 開車。

* speaker (ˈspikɚ) *n.* 說話者　　***according to*** 根據
map (mæp) *n.* 地圖　　road (rod) *n.* 道路
go to (路) 通往　　city (ˈsɪtɪ) *n.* 城市
wrong (rɔŋ) *adj.* 錯誤的　　way (we) *n.* 路；方向
I think so. 我想是的。　　stop (stɑp) *v.* 停止
gas station 加油站　　***ask for*** 請求
directions (dəˈrɛkʃənz) *n. pl.* 方向；指示　　hope (hop) *v.* 希望
help (hɛlp) *v.* 幫忙　　ride (raɪd) *v.* 搭乘
bus (bʌs) *n.* 公車　　fly (flaɪ) *v.* 駕駛 (飛機)
plane (plen) *n.* 飛機 (= *airplane*)
drive (draɪv) *v.* 開 (車)　　car (kɑr) *n.* 汽車

16. (**C**) Question : What was Robert's grade on the test?

問：羅伯特考試的成績如何？

W : Have you told your parents about the test, Robert?

女：你有告訴你父母關於考試的事情嗎，羅伯特？

M : No. They're going to be really angry.

男：沒有。他們會很生氣。

W : What happened? Didn't you study hard enough?

女：發生什麼事了？你讀書不夠用功嗎？

M : I guess not.

男：我想是不夠。

A. He got an A-plus. 他得到 A⁺。

B. He didn't take the test. 他沒有參加考試。

C. He got an F. 他考不及格。

* grade〔gred〕n. 成績　　test〔tɛst〕n. 考試
told〔told〕v. 告訴【tell 的過去式】
parents〔'pɛrənts〕n. pl. 父母　　Robert〔'rabət〕n. 羅伯特
really〔'riəlɪ〕adv. 確實；的確　　angry〔'æŋgrɪ〕adj. 生氣的
study〔'stʌdɪ〕v. 讀書　　hard〔hɑrd〕adv. 努力地
enough〔ɪ'nʌf〕adv. 足夠地　　guess〔gɛs〕v. 猜想；認為
A-plus A⁺（百分制的）96～100 分
take the test 參加考試　　F〔ɛf〕n. 不及格

17. (**A**)　Question : Do the speakers know each other?

問：說話者認識彼此嗎？

M : Hey, I'm Tim's cousin, Frank, from California.

男：嘿，我是提姆的表弟，法蘭克，來自美國加州。

W : Nice to meet you, Frank. I'm Laura, Tim's classmate.

女：很高興認識你，法蘭克。我是蘿拉，提姆的同班同學。

M : Nice to meet you, too. How long have you known Tim?

男：我也很高興認識妳。妳認識提姆多久了？

W : About five years.

女：大約五年。

A. No. They are meeting for the first time.

　不。他們第一次見面。

B. Yes. They are classmates. 是的。他們是同班同學。

C. No. They are cousins. 不。他們是表兄妹。

* *each other* 彼此　　hey〔he〕interj.（表示驚喜、喜悅、疑問等）嘿
Tim〔tɪm〕n. 提姆　　cousin〔'kʌzn〕n. 表（堂）兄弟姊妹
Frank〔fræŋk〕n. 法蘭克
California〔,kælə'fɔrnjə〕n.（美國）加州
Nice to meet you. 很高興認識你。　　Laura〔'lɔrə〕n. 蘿拉
classmate〔'klæs,met〕n. 同班同學
meet〔mit〕v. 見面；認識　　*for the first time* 生平第一次

18. (**B**) Question : What does the man say about Mr. Simon?

問：關於賽門先生男士說了什麼？

W : Mr. Simon isn't answering his phone. What should we do?

女：賽門先生沒有接電話。我們應該怎麼做？

M : He's always late. I think we should start without him.

男：他總是遲到。我想我們應該開始了，不管他。

W : Should we order something for him?

女：我們應該為他點些什麼嗎？

M : No, we don't know what he wants. Let him decide when he gets here.

男：不要，我們不知道他要什麼。當他到這裡再讓他自己決定。

A. He will order for him. 他會幫他點菜。

B. He's always late. 他總是遲到。

C. He always answers his phone. 他總是會接電話。

* Simon ('saɪmən) *n.* 賽門　　answer ('ænsə) *v.* 回應；接（電話）
phone (fon) *n.* 電話　　always ('ɔlwez) *adv.* 總是
late (let) *adj.* 遲到的　　start (stɑrt) *v.* 開始
without (wɪð'aut) *prep.* 沒有　　order ('ɔrdə) *v.* 點（菜）
decide (dɪ'saɪd) *v.* 決定　　get (gɛt) *v.* 到達

19. (**B**) Question : What does the woman want?

問：女士想要什麼？

M : What's wrong, Ann?

男：怎麼了，安？

W : Nothing.

女：沒事。

M : Did I say something wrong? Are you angry with me?

男：我說錯什麼了嗎？妳在對我生氣嗎？

W : No, I just don't feel like talking right now.

女：沒有，我只是現在不想說話。

A. She wants to talk with the man now.
　　她現在想要和男士講話。

B. She wants to be quiet. <u>她想要靜一靜。</u>

C. She wants to go to the doctor. 她想要去看醫生。

* ***What's wrong?*** 怎麼了？　　Ann〔æn〕*n.* 安
　be angry with *sb.* 對某人生氣　***feel like V-ing*** 想要～
　talk〔tɔk〕*v.* 說話　***right now*** 現在；目前
　quiet〔ˈkwaɪət〕*adj.* 安靜的　***go to the doctor*** 去看醫生

20.（ **A**) Question：Where does the man want to go?
　　問：男士要去哪裡？

M：Did you call a taxi for me?

男：妳有幫我叫計程車嗎？

W：No, but don't worry, Jimmy. Dad is on his way home right now.

女：沒有，不過別擔心，吉米。爸爸現在正在回家的路上。

M：I can't be late for this job interview, Mom. This is very important!

男：這個工作面試我不能遲到，媽。這很重要！

W：Don't worry. Dad will get you there on time.

女：別擔心。你爸會準時載你到那裡。

A. To a job interview. <u>去面試工作。</u>

B. To the airport. 去機場。

C. To his school. 去學校。

* call〔kɔl〕*v.* 叫（車）　　taxi〔ˈtæksɪ〕*n.* 計程車
　worry〔ˈwɝɪ〕*v.* 擔心　　Jimmy〔ˈdʒɪmɪ〕*n.* 吉米
　on *one's* ***way home*** 在回家途中　***right now*** 現在；目前
　job〔dʒɑb〕*n.* 工作　　interview〔ˈɪntɚˌvju〕*n.* 面試
　important〔ɪmˈpɔrtn̩t〕*adj.* 重要的　　get〔gɛt〕*v.* 使移動到
　on time 準時　　airport〔ˈɛrˌport〕*n.* 機場

TEST 5 詳解

聽力：是非題

1. (**Y**) The date is July 19th.
   日期是七月十九日。
   * date〔det〕*n.* 日期　　July〔dʒu'laɪ〕*n.* 七月

2. (**Y**) It is snowing.
   正在下雪。
   * snow〔sno〕*v.* 下雪

3. (**Y**) Fiona is riding a pony.

菲歐娜正騎著一隻小馬。

* Fiona〔 fɪˈonə 〕 *n.* 菲歐娜　　　ride〔 raɪd 〕 *v.* 騎
pony〔ˈponɪ 〕 *n.* 小馬

4. (**Y**) Jeff is good at math.

傑夫擅長數學。

* Jeff〔 dʒɛf 〕 *n.* 傑夫　　**be good at** 擅長
math〔 mæθ 〕 *n.* 數學

5. (**N**) Sue is wearing a sweater.

蘇穿著毛衣。

* wear〔wɛr〕v. 穿　　sweater〔'swɛtə〕n. 毛衣

6. (**Y**) They are eating healthy food.

他們正在吃健康的食物。

* healthy〔'hɛlθɪ〕adj. 健康的　　food〔fud〕n. 食物

7. (**N**) It is raining.

現在正在下雨。

* rain〔ren〕*v.* 下雨

8. (**Y**) Mr. Clark is on the telephone.

克拉克先生在講電話。

* Clark〔klɑrk〕*n.* 克拉克　　phone〔fon〕*n.* 電話
be on the phone 在講電話

9. (**N**) A man is sitting at the desk.

一名男士坐在書桌前。

* sit 〔 sɪt 〕 v. 坐　　at 〔 æt 〕 prep. 在…旁邊；靠近…
　desk 〔 dɛsk 〕 n. 書桌

10. (**N**) They are swimming in a river.

他們在河裡游泳。

* swim 〔 swɪm 〕 v. 游泳　　river 〔 'rɪvɚ 〕 n. 河流

聽力：選擇題

11. (**A**) Question : What is the problem?

問：問題是什麼？

W : Hi, William. What can I do for you?

女：嗨，威廉。我可以為你做什麼？

M : Hello, Debbie. I want to talk about your dog. It was barking all night.

男：哈囉，黛比。我想要說說關於妳的狗。牠整晚在叫。

W : I'm sorry about that, but he's a dog. Dogs bark at night sometimes. I don't know what else to do.

女：關於那件事我很抱歉，但是牠是隻狗。狗晚上偶爾會叫。我不知道我還能做些什麼。

M : Can't you keep him inside? He's very noisy.

男：妳不能把牠關在屋內嗎？牠很吵。

A. The woman's dog is too noisy. 女士的狗太吵。

B. The man lost his dog. 男士遺失他的狗。

C. The woman does not have a dog. 女士不想要養狗。

* problem〔'prɑbləm〕*n.* 問題　　William〔'wɪljəm〕*n.* 威廉
Debbie〔'dɛbɪ〕*n.* 黛比　　***talk about*** 談論
bark〔bɑrk〕*v.* 吠叫　　sometimes〔'sʌm͵taɪmz〕*adv.* 有時候；偶爾
else〔ɛls〕*adj.* 其他的　　keep〔kip〕*v.* 使處於
inside〔'ɪn'saɪd〕*adv.* 在屋內　　noisy〔'nɔɪzɪ〕*adj.* 吵的
lost〔lɔst〕*v.* 遺失【lose 的過去式】　　have〔hæv〕*v.* 養；飼養

12. (**B**) Question : What is Lisa doing?

問：莉莎正在做什麼？

M : Lisa, it's almost midnight.

男：莉莎，將近半夜了。

W : OK.

女：好的。

M : Turn off your computer and get ready for bed. Don't forget to brush your teeth.

男：關掉妳的電腦，然後準備上床睡覺。不要忘記刷牙。

W : In a minute, Dad. I want to put this picture on Facebook.

女：很快就好，爸爸。我想要把這張照片放到臉書。

A. Sleeping. 睡覺。

B. Using her computer. <u>使用她的電腦。</u>

C. Listening to music. 聽音樂。

* almost〔'ɔl,most〕adv. 幾乎；將近　　midnight〔'mɪd,naɪt〕n. 半夜
  turn off 關掉（電器）　　computer〔kəm'pjutɚ〕n. 電腦
  get ready for 準備好～　　bed〔bɛd〕n. 就寢
  forget〔fɚ'gɛt〕v. 忘記　　brush〔brʌʃ〕v. 刷
  teeth〔tiθ〕n. pl. 牙齒【單數為 tooth】　　minute〔'mɪnɪt〕n. 分鐘
  in a minute 馬上；很快（ = *very soon*）　　picture〔'pɪktʃɚ〕n. 照片
  Facebook〔'fes,bʊk〕n. 臉書【社交軟體】　　sleep〔slip〕v. 睡覺
  use〔juz〕v. 使用　　***listen to*** 聽　　music〔'mjuzɪk〕n. 音樂

13. (**B**) Question : Who is the man?

問：男士是誰？

W : How much is beef?

女：牛肉多少錢？

M : Five ninety-nine a pound.

男：一磅 5.99 美元。

W : Oh, that's too expensive.

女：喔，那太貴了。

M : I have chicken on sale for three ninety-nine a pound.

男：我有特價的雞肉，一磅 3.99 元美。

A. An artist. 一位藝術家。

B. A shopkeeper. <u>一位零售店老闆。</u>

C. A farmer. 一位農夫。

* beef〔bif〕n. 牛肉　　pound〔paʊnd〕n. 磅【1 磅等於 0.454 公斤】

oh〔o〕*interj.* （表示驚訝、恐懼等）喔；啊
expensive〔ɪkˋspɛnsɪv〕*adj.* 昂貴的   chicken〔ˋtʃɪkɪn〕*n.* 雞肉
on sale 特價中   artist〔ˋɑrtɪst〕*n.* 藝術家
shopkeeper〔ˋʃɑpˏkipɚ〕*n.* 零售店老闆   farmer〔ˋfɑrmɚ〕*n.* 農夫

14. (**C**) Question：How old is the girl?

問：女孩年紀多大？

M：You must be at least 12 years old to use the swimming
pool now.

男：妳至少要十二歲才能使用游泳池。

W：But I'm almost 12. I'm eleven years and ten months old.

女：但是我已經快要十二歲了。我現在是十一歲又十個月大。

M：I'm sorry. But you have to use the pool during the
children's swim time.

男：很抱歉。但是妳必須在孩童的游泳時段使用泳池。

W：Please! I'll be good. I promise.

女：拜託！我會很乖的。我保證。

A. She is 20 years old. 她二十歲。

B. She is 12 years old. 她十二歲。

C. She is 11 years old. 她十一歲。

* **at least** 至少   **swimming pool** 游泳池（= *pool*）
  month〔mʌnθ〕*n.* 月   **have to V.** 必須~
  during〔ˋdjʊrɪŋ〕*prep.* 在…期間
  children〔ˋtʃɪldrən〕*n. pl.* 小孩【單數為 child】
  good〔gʊd〕*adj.* 乖的；規矩的   promise〔ˋprɑmɪs〕*v.* 承諾；答應

15. (**C**) Question：Who is the man?

問：男士是誰？

M：Do you know why I stopped you?

男：你知道我為什麼攔下妳嗎？

W：Was I driving too fast?

女：是我開太快嗎？

M : Yes. You should drive only 60 kilometers per hour here. You were driving 80 kilometers. I have to give you a ticket.

男：是的。妳在這裡應該只能開時速六十公里。妳剛剛的時速是八十公里。我必須開妳罰單。

W : I'm sorry, officer.

女：我很抱歉，警官。

A. A bus driver.　一位公車司機。

B. A teacher.　一位老師。

C. A police officer.　一位警察。

* stop〔stɑp〕v. 停止；把⋯攔下　drive〔draɪv〕v. 開車
fast〔fæst〕adv. 快地　kilometer〔kɪˋlɑmɪtə〕n. 公里
per〔pə〕prep. 每⋯　hour〔aur〕n. 小時
ticket〔ˋtɪkɪt〕n. 罰單　officer〔ˋɔfəsə〕n. 警官；【用於稱呼】警察
driver〔ˋdraɪvə〕n. 駕駛人；司機　*police officer* 警察

16. (**C**) Question : What do we know about the man?

問：關於男士我們知道什麼？

W : Good to have you back, Bob. Everybody really missed you.

女：很高興你回到我們身邊，鮑伯。每個人都非常想念你。

M : Good to be back, Jane.

男：很高興可以回來，珍。

W : I'm sorry you were sick for so long.

女：你生病這麼久，我感到很遺憾。

M : Me, too, but I'm fine now.

男：我也是，不過我現在很健康。

A. He was on vacation.　他去度假。

B. He is a doctor.　他是一位醫生。

C. His was sick.　他生過病。

* *Good to V.* ～很好（= It's good to V.）

have sb. back 有某人回到身邊   Bob〔bɑb〕n. 鮑伯
miss〔mɪs〕v. 想念   Jane〔dʒen〕n. 珍
sorry〔'sɔrɪ〕adj. 遺憾的   sick〔sɪk〕adj. 生病的
for long 長久地   fine〔faɪn〕adj. 好的;健康的
on vacation 在休假;在度假   doctor〔'dɑktɚ〕n. 醫生

17. (**C**) Question : Why is the woman worried?

問:為何女士很擔心?

W : That's the third time Susie has called Gary tonight!

女:這是今晚蘇西第三次來找蓋瑞。

M : I guess she really likes him.

男:我想她真的喜歡他。

W : Gary is too young to have a girlfriend. Besides, he
needs to study hard.

女:蓋瑞還太小,不能有女朋友。此外,他需要用功讀書。

M : He's 15 years old and he's number one in his class. I
don't think Susie is a problem. She's a nice girl.

男:他十五歲了,而他是班上的第一名。我不認為蘇西是個問題。
她是個好女孩。

A. Her son has poor grades. 她的兒子成績不好。

B. She doesn't have a boyfriend. 她沒有男朋友。

C. Her son has a girlfriend. 她的兒子有女朋友。

* third〔θɝd〕adj. 第三的   time〔taɪm〕n. 次數
Susie〔'suzɪ〕n. 蘇西   call〔kɔl〕v. 打電話給(某人)
Gary〔'gærɪ〕n. 蓋瑞   guess〔gɛs〕v. 猜想;認為
like〔laɪk〕v. 喜歡   too…to V. 太…以致於不~
girlfriend〔'gɝl,frɛnd〕n. 女朋友   besides〔bɪ'saɪdz〕adv. 此外
need to V. 需要~   study hard 用功讀書
number one 第一名   class〔klæs〕n. 班級
nice〔naɪs〕adj. 好的   worried〔'wɝɪd〕adj. 擔心的
poor〔pʊr〕adj. 差勁的   grade〔gred〕n. 成績
boyfriend〔'bɔɪ,frɛnd〕n. 男朋友

18. (**B**) Question : What are the speakers talking about?

問：說話者在講談論什麼？

M : Do you ever buy things on the Internet?

男： 妳曾經在網路上買東西嗎？

W : Sometimes.　It's very convenient.

女： 有時候。非常方便。

M : I've never ordered anything online.　Is it difficult?

男： 我從來沒有在網路上訂購任何東西。這很困難嗎？

W : It's easy.　I can help you buy something online.

女： 很簡單。我可以幫助你在網路上買東西。

A. How much money they spend.　他們花了多少錢。

B. Shopping on the Internet.　<u>網路購物。</u>

C. Which department store to go to.　要去哪間百貨公司。

* ever ('ɛvɚ) *adv.* 曾經　　Internet ('ɪntɚ,nɛt) *n.* 網際網路
  convenient (kən'vinjənt) *adj.* 方便的　　order ('ɔrdɚ) *v.* 訂購
  online (,ɑn'laɪn) *adv.* 在網路上　　difficult ('dɪfə,kʌlt) *adj.* 困難的
  easy ('izɪ) *adj.* 簡單的　　spend (spɛnd) *v.* 花費
  shop (ʃɑp) *v.* 購物　　***department store*** 百貨公司

19. (**B**) Question : What will the man give Danny?

問：男士會給丹尼什麼？

W : Did you buy a gift for Danny's birthday yet?　I got him
a Super Soaker.　It's a type of water gun.

女： 你買了給丹尼的生日禮物了嗎？我買給他一個超級大雨。這是
一種水槍。

M : I haven't had time to get him anything.　I'll probably
just give him money in an envelope.

男： 我還沒有時間可以買東西給他。我可能只會用信封包錢給他。

W : I'm sure he'll like that.

女： 我確定他會喜歡那樣。

M : Money was my favorite type of birthday gift when I was
Danny's age.

男：錢是我在丹尼那個年紀時最喜愛的生日禮物。

A. A water gun. 一支水槍。

B. Money. 錢。

C. A birthday cake. 生日蛋糕。

* gift〔gɪft〕n. 禮物　　Danny〔'dænɪ〕n. 丹尼
birthday〔'bɝθ,de〕n. 生日　　yet〔jɛt〕adv.（用於疑問句）已經
got〔gɑt〕v. 幫（某人）買【get 的過去式】
soaker〔'sokɚ〕n. 傾盆大雨　　type〔taɪp〕n. 類型；種類
water gun 水槍　　probably〔'prɑbəblɪ〕adv. 可能
envelope〔'ɛnvə,lop〕n. 信封　　sure〔ʃʊr〕adj. 確定的
favorite〔'fevərɪt〕adj. 最喜愛的　　age〔edʒ〕n. 年紀
cake〔kek〕n. 蛋糕

20.（ **A** ）Question：What does the man want to do?

問：男士想要做什麼？

M：Excuse me. I want to buy this shirt.

男：對不起。我想要買這件襯衫。

W：OK. That will be three hundred dollars.

女：好的。那件是三百美元。

M：But the sign says that it is two hundred and fifty dollars.

男：但是標牌說這件是兩百五十美元。

W：Oh, you're right. I forgot that it was on sale.

女：喔，你說的對。我忘了這件在特價。

A. Buy a shirt. 買一件襯衫。

B. Pay three hundred dollars. 付三百美元。

C. Find a different shirt. 找一件不同的襯衫。

* **Excuse me**.（用於引起注意）對不起；很抱歉。
shirt〔ʃɝt〕n. 襯衫　　sign〔saɪn〕n. 招牌；標牌
say〔se〕v.（告示等）寫著；說　　right〔raɪt〕adj. 正確的
forgot〔fɚ'gɑt〕v. 忘記【forget 的過去式】　　pay〔pe〕v. 支付
find〔faɪnd〕v. 找到　　different〔'dɪfərənt〕adj. 不同的

TEST 6 詳解

聽力：是非題

1. (**N**) Bobby is carrying a suitcase.

　　巴比正提著一個手提箱。

　　* Bobby (ˈbɑbɪ) *n.* 巴比　　carry (ˈkærɪ) *v.* 攜帶；提著
　　suitcase (ˈsutˌkes) *n.* 手提箱

2. (**N**) Ms. Evans has made a batch of cookies.

　　埃文斯女士做了一批餅乾。

　　* Ms. (mɪz) *n.* 女士　　Evans (ˈɛvənz) *n.* 埃文斯
　　batch (bætʃ) *n.* 一批　　cookie (ˈkʊkɪ) *n.* 餅乾

3. (**N**) The cat is very skinny.

這隻貓很瘦。

* cat〔kæt〕*n.* 貓　　skinny〔ˈskɪnɪ〕*adj.* 很瘦的

4. (**N**) The boy is drawing on the wall.

男孩正在牆壁上畫圖。

* draw〔drɔ〕*v.* 畫圖　　wall〔wɔl〕*n.* 牆壁

5. (**Y**) Kevin is a student.

凱文是個學生。

* Kevin〔ˈkɛvɪn〕 *n.* 凱文　　student〔ˈstjudṇt〕 *n.* 學生

6. (**Y**) Mr. Taylor is a baseball coach.

泰勒先生是棒球教練。

* Mr.〔ˈmɪstɚ〕 *n.* 先生　　Taylor〔ˈtelɚ〕 *n.* 泰勒
baseball〔ˈbesˌbɔl〕 *n.* 棒球　　coach〔kotʃ〕 *n.* 教練

7. (**N**) Mary is a teacher.

瑪麗是位老師。

＊ teacher〔ˈtitʃɚ〕*n.* 老師

8. (**Y**) Tom is a crossing guard.

湯姆是交通警察。

＊ crossing〔ˈkrɔsɪŋ〕*n.* 十字路口；行人穿越道
guard〔gɑrd〕*n.* 警衛　　*crossing guard* 交通警察

9. (**N**) The sun is shining.

陽光燦爛。

* sun〔sʌn〕*n.* 太陽　　shine〔ʃaɪn〕*v.* 發光；照耀

10. (**N**) There are four passengers in the car.

車上有四位乘客。

* **there** + **be** 有～　　passenger〔'pæsṇdʒɚ〕*n.* 乘客
car〔kɑr〕*n.* 汽車

聽力：選擇題

11. (**B**) Question : Who is the girl?

　　問：那女孩是誰？

　　M : You're the new student Mr. Wang was talking about, aren't you?

　　男：妳是王老師說的那位新來的學生吧，不是嗎？

　　W : I don't know. It is my first day, though. My name is Linda.

　　女：我不知道。不過今天是我第一天到這。我的名字是琳達。

　　M : Nice to meet you, Linda. Where are you from?

　　男：很高興認識妳，琳達。妳來自哪裡？

　　W : Singapore.

　　女：新加坡。

　　A. An old friend. 一位老朋友。

　　B. A new student. <u>一位新來的學生。</u>

　　C. A popular teacher. 一位受歡迎的老師。

　　* new〔nju〕*adj.* 新的；剛到的　　though〔ðo〕*adv.* 然而；不過
　　　Linda〔'lɪndə〕*n.* 琳達　　***Nice to meet you.*** 很高興認識你。
　　　Singapore〔'sɪŋgə,por〕*n.* 新加坡　　popular〔'pɑpjələ〕*adj.* 受歡迎的

12. (**B**) Question : Why is Scott's mother angry?

　　問：為何史考特的媽媽很生氣？

　　W : Scott, what are you doing?

　　女：史考特，你在做什麼？

　　M : I'm making a sandwich, Mom.

　　男：我在做三明治，媽。

　　W : How many times have I told you to take off your shoes before you come in the house? Now there's mud all over my carpet.

　　女：我跟你說過多少次，進門要脫鞋？現在我的地毯都是泥巴。

M：Sorry, Mom. I forgot.

男：很抱歉，媽。我忘記了。

A. Scott is eating a sandwich. 史考特正在吃三明治。

B. Scott didn't take off his shoes. 史考特沒有脫鞋。

C. Scott came home late. 史考特晚回家。

* Scott〔skɑt〕n. 史考特　　angry〔'æŋgrɪ〕adj. 生氣的
sandwich〔'sændwɪtʃ〕n. 三明治　　time〔taɪm〕n. 次數
take off 脫掉　　shoes〔ʃuz〕n. pl. 鞋子　　mud〔mʌd〕n. 泥巴
all over 遍及　　carpet〔'kɑrpɪt〕n. 地毯
forgot〔fə'gɑt〕v. 忘記【forget 的過去式】　　late〔let〕adv. 晚

13. (**C**) Question : When will the woman come back?

問：女士何時會回來？

M：You've worked very hard, May. I want you to take a rest.

男：妳已經工作很努力了，梅。我要妳休息一下。

W：I can't, Mr. Peterson. I have to finish these reports.

女：我不行，彼得森先生。我必須完成這些報告。

M：Forget about the reports. They'll be here tomorrow. You should go home.

男：不要再想著這些報告。它們明天還會在這裡。你應該回家了。

W：Thanks, Mr. Peterson. I'll see you first thing in the morning.

女：謝謝，彼得森先生。明天一早見。

A. She will stay. 她會留下來。

B. This afternoon. 今天下午。

C. Tomorrow morning. 明天早上。

* work〔wɝk〕v. 工作　　hard〔hɑrd〕adv. 努力地
May〔me〕n. 梅　　rest〔rɛst〕n. 休息　　**take a rest** 休息一下
Peterson〔'pitəsən〕n. 彼得森　　**have to V.** 必須～
finish〔'fɪnɪʃ〕v. 完成　　report〔rɪ'port〕n. 報告
forget about 忘記；不要把⋯放在心上

the first thing in the morning 早起的第一件事；一早
stay〔ste〕*v.* 留下來

14. (**C**) Question：Why does Julie feel sad?

問：為何茱莉感到難過？

M：I heard Julie's cat died last week. What was its name?

男：我聽說茱莉的貓上禮拜死了。牠的名字是什麼？

W：Rex. She loved that cat. She's very sad.

女：雷克斯。她很愛那隻貓。她現在非常難過。

M：I know how it feels to lose a pet. It really hurts.

男：我知道失去寵物的感受。真的讓人很傷心。

W：Me, too. Our dog, Sampson, died last year. It was heartbreaking.

女：我也是。去年我們的狗，山普森，死了。這真讓人心痛。

A. She hurt herself. 她受傷了。

B. She is in the hospital. 她現在在醫院。

C. Her cat died. 她的貓死了。

* heard〔hɜd〕*v.* 聽說【hear 的過去式】　　Julie〔'dʒulɪ〕*n.* 茱莉
die〔daɪ〕*v.* 死　　Rex〔rɛks〕*n.* 雷克斯　　sad〔sæd〕*adj.* 悲傷的
lose〔luz〕*v.* 失去　　pet〔pɛt〕*n.* 寵物
hurt〔hɜt〕*v.* 疼痛；使人傷心　　Sampson〔'sæmpsən〕*n.* 山普森
heartbreaking〔'hɑrt,brekɪŋ〕*adj.* 令人心碎的；令人心痛的
hurt *oneself* 受傷　　hospital〔'hɑspɪtl̩〕*n.* 醫院

15. (**B**) Question：What is the man doing?

問：男士正在做什麼？

W：Would you mind turning down your radio? I'm trying to study.

女：你介意把你收音機關小聲嗎？我現在要讀書。

M：I'm sorry. I didn't know it was too loud. I'll close my door.

男：我很抱歉。我不知道這太大聲了。我會把門關上。

W : Please do. With the door open, I can hear the music all the way in my bedroom.

女：拜託你。門打開著，我在臥室裡可以完全聽得到音樂聲。

M : I can turn it down a little, too.

男：我也可以關小聲一點。

A. Studying. 讀書。
B. Listening to music. 聽音樂。
C. Watching TV. 看電視。

* mind〔maɪnd〕v. 介意　　***turn down*** 關小聲
　radio〔'redɪ,o〕n. 收音機　　study〔'stʌdɪ〕v. 讀書
　loud〔laʊd〕adj. 大聲的　　close〔kloz〕v. 關
　open〔'opən〕adj. 打開的　　***all the way*** 一路上；完全
　bedroom〔'bɛd,rum〕n. 臥室　　***a little*** 一點點　　***listen to*** 聽
　music〔'mjuzɪk〕n. 音樂　　***watch TV*** 看電視

16. (**B**) Question : Does the man like Larry Smith?

問：男士喜歡賴瑞・史密斯嗎？

M : Oh, no. Here comes Larry Smith. I was really hoping he wouldn't be here tonight.

男：喔，不。賴瑞・史密斯來了。我眞希望他今晚不要在這。

W : What's wrong with Larry Smith? He's one of George's best friends.

女：賴瑞・史密斯怎麼了？他是喬治最好的朋友之一。

M : I don't like him.

男：我不喜歡他。

W : I think he's nice and handsome. And George likes him a lot.

女：我覺得他人很好又英俊。而且喬治很喜歡他。

A. He thinks Larry is nice. 他覺得賴瑞人很好。
B. No, he doesn't. 不，他不喜歡。
C. He likes Larry a lot. 他很喜歡賴瑞。

* Larry Smith 〔ˈlærɪ smɪθ 〕*n.* 賴瑞・史密斯　　hope 〔 hop 〕*v.* 希望
What's wrong with ~ ? ~ 怎麼了；~ 有什麼問題？
George 〔 dʒɔrdʒ 〕*n.* 喬治　　handsome 〔ˈhænsəm 〕*adj.* 英俊的
a lot 非常 (*= very much*)

17. (**C**) Question : What is the girl worried about?

問：小女孩在擔心什麼？

W : Dad, there's a strange dog in our front yard.

女：爸爸，我們家前院有一隻奇怪的狗。

M : What does it look like?

男：那隻狗看起來如何？

W : It's black with white spots.

女：黑色帶有白色斑點。

M : Oh, that's the Morgans' dog. Don't worry about him.
　　He's not dangerous.

男：喔，那是摩根家的狗。不用擔心牠。牠不危險。

A. A strange man at the door. 門口陌生的男人。

B. A loud noise in the bathroom. 浴室裡很大的噪音。

C. A dog in the front yard. <u>前院的狗。</u>

* strange 〔 strendʒ 〕*adj.* 奇怪的；陌生的　　front 〔 frʌnt 〕*adj.* 前面的
yard 〔 jɑrd 〕*n.* 院子　　look 〔 luk 〕*n.* 看起來
black 〔 blæk 〕*adj.* 黑色的　　white 〔 hwaɪt 〕*adj.* 白色的
spot 〔 spɑt 〕*n.* 斑點　　Morgan 〔ˈmɔrgən 〕*n.* 摩根
the Morgans 摩根一家人　　worry 〔ˈwɝɪ 〕*v.* 擔心；煩惱 < *about* >
dangerous 〔ˈdendʒərəs 〕*adj.* 危險的　　***be worried about*** 擔心
at the door 在門口　　noise 〔 nɔɪz 〕*n.* 噪音
bathroom 〔ˈbæθˌrum 〕*n.* 浴室

18. (**B**) Question : What did the woman do in Hualien?

問：這位女士在花蓮做了什麼？

M : Did you enjoy your trip to Hualien?

男：妳去花蓮的旅行愉快嗎？

W : I sure did. We went hiking and swimming, and ate a lot of delicious food.

女：當然。我們去遠足和游泳，而且吃了很多好吃的食物。

M : Sounds like fun. How long were you there?

男：聽起來很有趣。妳在那邊多久？

W : For three days. I wish it could have been longer. I loved it there.

女：三天。我希望可以久一點。我很喜歡那裡。

A. She went shopping. 她去購物。

B. She went hiking and swimming. <u>她去遠足和游泳。</u>

C. She went fishing. 她去釣魚。

* enjoy 〔ɪn'dʒɔɪ〕 v. 喜愛；享受   trip 〔trɪp〕 n. 旅行
  Hualien 〔'hwɑljən〕 n. 花蓮   sure 〔ʃʊr〕 adv. 的確；當然
  go + V-ing 去~   hike 〔haɪk〕 v. 健行；遠足
  swim 〔swɪm〕 v. 游泳   ate 〔et〕 v. 吃【eat 的過去式】
  a lot of 很多   delicious 〔dɪ'lɪʃəs〕 adj. 美味的；好吃的
  food 〔fud〕 n. 食物   sound 〔saʊnd〕 v. 聽起來
  fun 〔fʌn〕 n. 有趣的事
  Sounds like fun. 聽起來很有趣。(= It sounds like fun.)
  wish 〔wɪʃ〕 v. 希望   **could have p.p.** 當時可以~
  love it there 喜歡那裡 (= love that place)
  shop 〔ʃɑp〕 v. 購物   fish 〔fɪʃ〕 v. 釣魚

19. (**C**) Question : How much does the scarf cost?

問：圍巾要多少錢？

W : How much is this scarf?

女：這條圍巾多少錢？

M : That one is $950.

男：那條要美金 950 元。

W : That's so expensive!

女：那真昂貴！

M : It's expensive because it was made in France.

男：這很貴，因為是法國製的。

A. Four hundred dollars. 四百美元。

B. It's not expensive. 它不貴。

C. $950. 九百五十美元。

* scarf〔skɑrf〕*n.* 圍巾　expensive〔ɪk'spɛnsɪv〕*adj.* 昂貴的
  made〔med〕*v.* 製作【make 的過去分詞】
  France〔fræns〕*n.* 法國　cost〔kɔst〕*v.* 值（多少錢）

20. (**C**) Question : What are the speakers talking about?

問：說話者在談論什麼？

M : Here's Tommy's backpack, and here is his lunch.
Here is the money for his field trip to the zoo.

男：這是湯米的背包，這是他的午餐。這是他去動物園戶外教學
的錢。

W : Does he have a sweater?

女：他有毛衣嗎？

M : He won't need a sweater. It will be sunny and warm
all day.

男：他不會需要毛衣。天氣會是整天都晴朗且溫暖。

W : Maybe. The weather can change very quickly.

女：或許吧。天氣可能很快就會改變。

A. Their school. 他們的學校。

B. Their vacation. 他們的假期。

C. Their son, Tommy. 他們的兒子，湯米。

* speaker〔'spikɚ〕*n.* 說話者　Tommy〔'tɑmɪ〕*n.* 湯米
  backpack〔'bæk,pæk〕*n.* 背包　lunch〔lʌntʃ〕*n.* 午餐
  field〔fild〕*n.* 田野　*field trip* 戶外教學　zoo〔zu〕*n.* 動物園
  sweater〔'swɛtɚ〕*n.* 毛衣　sunny〔'sʌnɪ〕*adj.* 晴朗的
  warm〔wɔrm〕*adj.* 溫暖的　*all day* 整天
  maybe〔'mebi〕*adv.* 或許；可能　weather〔'wɛðɚ〕*n.* 天氣
  change〔tʃendʒ〕*v.* 改變　quickly〔'kwɪklɪ〕*adv.* 快速地
  vacation〔ve'keʃən〕*n.* 假期　son〔sʌn〕*n.* 兒子

TEST 7 詳解

聽力：是非題

1. (**Y**) This is a skirt.

　　　這是一件裙子。

　　　* skirt〔skɝt〕n. 裙子

2. (**Y**) The boys are running a race.

　　　男孩們正在賽跑。

　　　* run〔rʌn〕v. 跑；參加（賽跑）　　race〔res〕n. 賽跑；比賽
　　　run a race 賽跑

3. (**Y**) It is someone's birthday.

今天是某人的生日。

* birthday (ˈbɝθˌde) *n.* 生日

4. (**Y**) Danny is decorating the tree.

丹尼正在佈置樹。

* decorate (ˈdɛkəˌret) *v.* 裝飾；佈置
tree (tri) *n.* 樹

5. (Y) It is Saturday at 2:30.

現在是星期六的二點三十分。

　　* Saturday (ˈsætɚde) n. 星期六

6. (Y) There are English books on the desk.

書桌上有幾本英文書。

　　* *there + be* 有～　　English (ˈɪŋglɪʃ) adj. 英語的
　　book (bʊk) n. 書　　desk (dɛsk) n. 書桌

7. (**N**) This is a radio.

這是一台收音機。

* radio (ˈredɪˌo) *n.* 收音機

8. (**N**) They are watching a movie.

他們在看電影。

* watch (watʃ) *v.* 注視；觀看　　movie (ˈmuvɪ) *n.* 電影

9. (Y) She is playing with a cat.

她正在跟貓玩。

* play〔ple〕v. 玩   cat〔kæt〕n. 貓

10. (Y) There are three pencils.

有三枝鉛筆。

* pencil〔'pɛnsḷ〕n. 鉛筆

聽力：選擇題

11. (**B**) Question : What is the man doing?

問：男士在做什麼？

W : Do you like the pie, David?

女：你喜歡那個派嗎，大衛？

M : Yes. It's so delicious!

男：是的。這很好吃！

W : Maybe I should have some.

女：或許我應該吃一點。

M : Please do. I'm afraid I'm going to eat the whole thing!

男：請吃。我恐怕要把全部都吃完了！

A. Cooking dinner. 煮晚餐。

B. Eating a piece of pie. 吃一片派。

C. Cleaning up the kitchen. 打掃廚房。

* pie〔paɪ〕*n.* 派　　David〔'devɪd〕*n.* 大衛
delicious〔dɪ'lɪʃəs〕*adj.* 好吃的；美味的
maybe〔'mebi〕*adv.* 或許；可能　　have〔hæv〕*v.* 吃
I'm afraid 我恐怕　　whole〔hol〕*adj.* 全部的
cook〔kʊk〕*v.* 煮；烹調　　dinner〔'dɪnɚ〕*n.* 晚餐
clean up 打掃　　kitchen〔'kɪtʃɪn〕*n.* 廚房

12. (**B**) Question : Why are the speakers worried?

問：為什麼說話者很擔心？

M : What was that noise?

男：那噪音是什麼？

W : I think another bird flew into the window. At least, that's what it sounded like.

女：我想是又有一隻鳥撞上了窗戶。至少聽起來像是那樣。

M : Again? Is it dead?

男：又一次？那隻鳥死掉了嗎？

W : I don't know. Go outside and look.

女：我不知道。去外面看看。

A. They smelled smoke. 他們聞到煙味。

B. They heard a loud noise. <u>他們聽到很大的噪音。</u>

C. They saw a stranger at the door.

　　他們看到有個陌生人在門口。

* speaker (ˈspikɚ) n. 說話者　　worried (ˈwɝɪd) adj. 擔心的
  noise (nɔɪz) n. 噪音　　bird (bɝd) n. 鳥
  flew (flu) v. 飛【fly 的過去式】　　into (ˈɪntə) prep. 撞上
  window (ˈwɪndo) n. 窗戶；窗玻璃　　**at least** 至少
  sound (saʊnd) v. 聽起來　　again (əˈgɛn) adv. 又一次；再一次
  dead (dɛd) adj. 死的　　outside (ˈaʊtˈsaɪd) adv. 到外面
  smell (smɛl) v. 聞到…的味道　　smoke (smok) n. 煙
  heard (hɝd) v. 聽到【hear 的過去式】
  loud (laʊd) adj. 大聲的　　saw (sɔ) v. 看到【see 的過去式】
  stranger (ˈstrendʒɚ) n. 陌生人　　**at the door** 在門口

13. (**C**) Question : Who is Champ?

　　問：錢普是誰？

W : Jim, did you remember to feed Champ?

女：吉姆，你有記得餵錢普嗎？

M : Yes, Mom.

男：有的，媽。

W : Did you also remember to let him out in the backyard?

女：你也有記得要放牠出來到後院嗎？

M : Yes. And I made sure the gate was locked.

男：有的。而且我有確定大門是鎖著的。

A. A friend. 一位朋友。

B. A family member. 一位家庭成員。

C. A pet. <u>一隻寵物。</u>

* Jim (dʒɪm) n. 吉姆　　remember (rɪˈmɛmbɚ) v. 記得

feed〔fid〕v. 餵　　Champ〔tʃæmp〕n. 錢普
let out 放出；釋放　　backyard〔'bæk,jɑrd〕n. 後院
make sure 確認　　gate〔get〕n. 大門
lock〔lɑk〕v. 鎖　　friend〔frɛnd〕n. 朋友
member〔'mɛmbɚ〕n. 成員　　pet〔pɛt〕n. 寵物

14.（**A**）Question：Why was the man late?

問：男士爲何遲到？

M：How long have you been waiting?

男：你等多久了？

W：Only a few minutes. I was late, too.

女：只有幾分鐘。我也遲到了。

M：Good. Sorry about that. Traffic was very bad.

男：好的。眞抱歉。交通很糟糕。

W：I know! It must be because of the rain.

女：我知道！一定是因爲下雨。

A. The traffic was bad. 交通狀況不佳。

B. He forgot the date. 他忘記日期。

C. His car did not start. 他的車子無法發動。

* wait〔wet〕v. 等待　　**a few** 一些
minute〔'mɪnɪt〕n. 分鐘　　late〔let〕adj. 遲到的
sorry〔'sɔrɪ〕adj. 抱歉的　　traffic〔'træfɪk〕n. 交通
bad〔bæd〕adj. 不好的　　must〔mʌst〕aux. 一定
because of 因爲　　rain〔ren〕n. 下雨
forgot〔fɚ'gɑt〕v. 忘記【forget 的過去式】　　date〔det〕n. 日期
car〔kɑr〕n. 汽車　　start〔stɑrt〕v. 發動

15.（**A**）Question：What will the speakers do this weekend?

問：說話者這個週末會做什麼？

W：There's a movie festival in Grant Park this weekend, Larry.

女：格蘭特公園這個週末有電影節，賴瑞。

M : Hmm. Sounds interesting. Are you going?

男：嗯。聽起來很有趣。妳要去嗎？

W : I really want to go, but I can't find anyone to go with me.
　　I don't want to go alone. Maybe we could go together?

女：我真的很想去，但是我找不到人跟我一起去。我不想一個人
　　去。或許我們可以一起去？

M : That would be great!

男：那太棒了！

A. Go to a movie festival. 去參加電影節。

B. Go shopping. 去購物。

C. Visit another country. 遊覽另一個國家。

* movie (ˈmuvɪ) n. 電影　　festival (ˈfɛstəvḷ) n. 節慶
　Grant (grænt) n. 格蘭特　　park (pɑrk) n. 公園
　weekend (ˈwikˈɛnd) n. 週末　　Larry (ˈlærɪ) n. 賴瑞
　hmm (hm) interj. (表示懷疑、停頓等) 唔；嗯
　sound (saund) adj. 聽起來　　interesting (ˈɪntrɪstɪŋ) adj. 有趣的
　Sound interesting. 聽起來有趣的。(= *It sounds interesting.*)
　find (faɪnd) v. 找到　　alone (əˈlon) adv. 獨自
　maybe (ˈmebɪ) adv. 或許；可能　　great (gret) adj. 很棒的
　go + V-ing 去~　　shop (ʃɑp) v. 購物
　visit (ˈvɪzɪt) v. 探訪；遊覽　　country (ˈkʌntrɪ) n. 國家

16. (**C**) Question：How does Amy feel about her summer vacation?

問：艾美覺得她的暑假如何？

M : How was your summer vacation, Amy?

男：妳的暑假如何，艾美？

W : Too short, Tom.

女：太短了，湯姆。

M : I know what you mean. Six weeks is not long enough.

男：我知道妳的意思。六週不夠長。

W : I liked it better in junior high when we had eight weeks'
　　vacation.

女：我比較喜歡我們在國中的時候，有八週的假期。

A. It was too long. 太長了。

B. It was too hot. 太熱了。

C. It was too short. 太短了。

* Amy (ˈæmɪ) n. 艾美　　summer (ˈsʌmɚ) n. 夏天
  vacation (veˈkeʃən) n. 假期　　short (ʃɔrt) adj. 短的
  mean (min) v. 意思是　　like ~ better 更喜歡~
  like it when S. + V. 喜歡…的時候【it 為虛受詞，代替後面 when 引導的
  名詞子句】
  junior high 國中 (= junior high school)　　hot (hɑt) adj. 熱的

17. (**B**) Question：Where does the woman want to go?

問：女士想要去哪裡？

W：Do you know if this bus goes to the zoo?

女：你知道這部公車是否有到動物園嗎？

M：I think it does, but you should ask the driver.

男：我想是有的，但是妳應該問司機。

W：Thank you. I'll ask him.

女：謝謝你。我會問他。

M：You're welcome. Good luck! I hope you can find
   your way to the zoo.

男：不客氣。祝妳好運！希望妳能找到去動物園的路。

A. To the museum. 去博物館。

B. To the zoo. 去動物園。

C. To the bank. 去銀行。

* bus (bʌs) n. 公車　　zoo (zu) n. 動物園
  ask (æsk) v. 問　　driver (ˈdraɪvɚ) n. 司機；駕駛
  You're welcome. 不客氣。　　Good luck! 祝你好運！
  find (faɪnd) v. 找到　　way to… 通往…的路
  museum (mjuˈziəm) n. 博物館　　bank (bæŋk) n. 銀行

18. (**B**) Question : Does the man like the woman's dress?

問：男士喜歡女士的洋裝嗎？

M : Is that a new dress?

男：那是新的洋裝嗎？

W : Yes, it is. Do you like it?

女：是的。你喜歡嗎？

M : Sure, I like it a lot.

男：當然，我很喜歡。

W : What do you think of these shoes?

女：你覺得這雙鞋如何？

A. No, he doesn't. 不，他不喜歡。

B. Yes, he does. 是的，他喜歡。

C. It's impossible to say. 不知道。

* new (nju) *adj.* 新的　　dress (drɛs) *n.* 洋裝
sure (ʃur) *adv.* 當然　　*a lot* 非常 (= *very much*)
think of 覺得；認為　　shoes (ʃuz) *n. pl.* 鞋子
impossible (ɪm'pasəbl) *adj.* 可能的
It's impossible to say. 不知道；很難說。

19. (**C**) Question : What time does George need to leave the house?

問：喬治必須何時出門？

W : What time do you have to work, George?

女：你必須幾點工作，喬治？

M : I start at four p.m., so I need to leave the house around three.

男：我下午四點開始，所以我需要在三點左右出門。

W : What time do you finish your work?

女：你幾點結束工作？

M : Just after midnight.

男：就在午夜過後。

A. Midnight. 午夜。

B. 4:00 a.m. 上午四點。

C. 3:00 p.m. 下午三點。

* ***have to V.*** 必須～   work〔wɜk〕*v. n.* 工作

  Gorge〔dʒɔrdʒ〕*n.* 喬治   start〔stɑrt〕*v.* 開始

  p.m. 午後；下午（= *post meridiem*）   leave〔liv〕*v.* 離開

  around〔əˋraʊnd〕*prep.* 大約   finish〔ˋfɪnɪʃ〕*v.* 結束；完成

  midnight〔ˋmɪd͵naɪt〕*n.* 午夜【晚上十二點】

  a.m. 午前；上午（= *ante meridiem*）

20.（ **B** ）Question：Who left the back door open?

  問：誰讓後門打開？

  M：Is there a reason the back door is open?

  男：後門是開著的，有什麼理由嗎？

  W：Yes, I was in the garden when the phone rang. I came in,
     but I forgot to close the door.

  女：有的，當電話響時，我正在花園。我進門，但是忘了關門。

  M：Can I close it? I don't want the cat to get out.

  男：我可以把門關上嗎？我不想要讓貓跑出去。

  W：Sure.

  女：當然。

  A. The man. 男士。

  B. The woman. 女士。

  C. The cat. 貓。

* left〔lɛft〕*v.* 使處於（某種狀態）【leave 的過去式】

  back door 後門   open〔ˋopən〕*adj.* 開著的；打開的

  reason〔ˋrizn̩〕*n.* 理由；原因

  garden〔ˋgɑrdn̩〕*n.* 花園   phone〔fon〕*n.* 電話

  rang〔ræŋ〕*v.* 鈴響【ring 的過去式】

  forgot〔fəˋgɑt〕*v.* 忘記【forget 的過去式】   close〔kloz〕*v.* 關上

  cat〔kæt〕*n.* 貓   ***get out*** 離開；外出   sure〔ʃʊr〕*adv.* 當然

TEST 8 詳解

聽力：是非題

1. (**N**) The frogs are dancing.

青蛙正在跳舞。

* frog〔frɑg〕*n.* 青蛙　　dance〔dæns〕*v.* 跳舞

2. (**Y**) The boys are talking on the phone.

男孩們正在講電話。

* *on the phone* 用電話　　*talk on the phone* 講電話

3. (**N**) This is a guitar.

　　這是一把吉他。

　　* guitar〔gɪˋtɑr〕*n.* 吉他

4. (**Y**) The window is open.

　　窗戶是開著的。

　　* window〔ˋwɪndo〕*n.* 窗戶　　open〔ˋopən〕*adj.* 打開的;開著的

5. (**N**) This is a flag.

這是一面國旗。

* flag〔flæg〕*n.* 旗；國旗

6. (**Y**) The students are learning math.

學生們正在學數學。

* student〔'stjudn̩t〕*n.* 學生　　learn〔lɝn〕*v.* 學習
math〔mæθ〕*n.* 數學

7. (**N**) This is an animal.

　　　這是一隻動物。

　　　* animal〔'ænəml̩〕*n.* 動物

8. (**Y**) Ms. Hudson is preparing some food.

　　　哈德遜女士正在準備一些食物。

　　　* Ms.〔mɪz〕*n.* 女士　　　Hudson〔'hʌdsən〕*n.* 哈德遜

　　　prepare〔prɪ'pɛr〕*v.* 準備　　　food〔fud〕*n.* 食物

9. (**N**) The girls are playing soccer.

女孩們正在踢足球。

* soccer〔'sakɚ〕*n.* 足球　　***play soccer*** 踢足球

10. (**N**) Some books are stacked on a table.

有些書被堆放在桌子上。

* book〔bʊk〕*n.* 書　　stack〔stæk〕*v.* 堆放
   table〔'tebl̩〕*n.* 桌子

聽力：選擇題

11. (**B**) Question : When will they go swimming?

問：他們何時會去游泳？

W : Would you like to go swimming tomorrow afternoon?

女：你明天下午想去游泳嗎？

M : Sure, but I need to ask my dad first. I'm sure he'll say yes.

男：當然，但是我需要先問我爸。我確定他會說好。

W : OK, meet me at the park around noon. We can ride our bikes to the swimming pool.

女：好，大約中午在公園和我見面。我們可以騎腳踏車去游泳池。

M : If I can't go, I'll call you.

男：如果我無法去的話，我會打電話給妳。

A. Tomorrow morning. 明天早上。

B. Tomorrow afternoon. 明天下午。

C. Tomorrow evening. 明天傍晚。

* *go swimming* 去游泳　　*would like to V*. 想要～
tomorrow〔tə'mɔro〕*n.* 明天　　afternoon〔,æftə'nun〕*n.* 下午
sure〔ʃur〕*adv.* 當然　*adj.* 確定的　　need〔nid〕*v.* 必須
first〔fɜst〕*adv.* 首先　　meet〔mit〕*v.* 和～見面
park〔pɑrk〕*n.* 公園　　around〔ə'raund〕*prep.* 大約
noon〔nun〕*n.* 中午　　ride〔raid〕*v.* 騎　　bike〔baik〕*n.* 腳踏車
pool〔pul〕*n.* 游泳池　　call〔kɔl〕*v.* 打電話給
morning〔'mɔrnɪŋ〕*n.* 早上　　evening〔'ivənɪŋ〕*n.* 傍晚

12. (**A**) Question : Has the girl finished her homework?

問：女孩完成她的功課了嗎？

M : Have you finished your homework?

男：妳已經完成你的功課了嗎？

W : Not yet. I haven't finished my English assignment.

女：還沒。我還沒完成我的英語作業。

M : You should do that now before it gets too late.

　　I don't want you staying up past midnight again.

男：妳應該現在就要做，在還沒太晚之前。我不希望妳又再熬夜到

　　超過晚上十二點。

W : I can finish it on the bus tomorrow morning.

女：我可以明天早上在公車上完成。

A. No, she hasn't. 不，她還沒。

B. Yes, she has. 是的，她完成了。

C. I don't know. 我不知道。

* finish〔ˈfɪnɪʃ〕*v.* 完成　　homework〔ˈhomˌwɝk〕*n.* 功課

　not yet 還沒　　English〔ˈɪŋglɪʃ〕*adj.* 英語的

　assignment〔əˈsaɪnmənt〕*n.* 作業　　get〔gɛt〕*v.* 變得

　late〔let〕*adj.* 晚的；遲的　　want〔wɑnt〕*v.* 希望

　stay up 熬夜　　past〔pæst〕*prep.* 超過

　midnight〔ˈmɪdˌnaɪt〕*n.* 午夜【晚上十二點】

　again〔əˈgɛn〕*adv.* 再一次　　bus〔bʌs〕*n.* 公車

13. (**A**) Question : How much does the ferry boat cost on Wednesday?

問：在禮拜三搭乘渡輪要多少錢？

W : How much does a boat ticket cost?

女：船票要多少錢？

M : On weekdays it's fifty dollars, each way.

男：平日一個人單程五十美元。

W : What about weekends?

女：那週末呢？

M : It's sixty dollars on weekends and holidays.

男：週末和假日是六十美元。

A. 50 dollars each way. 單程五十美元。

B. 120 dollars. 一百二十美元。

C. 60 dollars each way. 單程六十美元。

* ferry〔ˈfɛrɪ〕*n.* 渡輪　　boat〔bot〕*n.* 船

cost〔kɔst〕*v.* 花費　　ticket〔'tɪkɪt〕*n.* 票
weekday〔'wik,de〕*n.* 平日　　*each way* 單程；一趟
What about…? …如何？　　weekend〔'wik'ɛnd〕*n.* 週末
holiday〔'hɑlə,de〕*n.* 假日　　Wednesday〔'wɛnzde〕*n.* 禮拜三

14. (**A**) Question：How often does the woman eat at the restaurant?

問：女士多常在這家餐廳吃飯？

W：Do you come here often?

女：你常來這裡嗎？

M：Not really. I stop in once a month or so. How about you?

男：不完全是。我大約一個月順路來一次。妳呢？

W：Me? I come here a lot. I've been eating here five times a week for the last 10 years.

女：我？我是常客。在過去的十年內，我一週在這裡吃飯五次。

M：Wow, what a good customer. The owners must love you.

男：哇，妳真是個好顧客。老闆一定很愛妳。

A. Often. <u>經常。</u>

B. Sometimes. 偶爾。

C. Seldom. 很少。

* ***how often*** 多常；多久一次　　restaurant〔'rɛstərənt〕*n.* 餐廳
often〔'ɔfən〕*adv.* 常常　　***not really*** 不完全是
stop in 順便拜訪　　once〔wʌns〕*adv.* 一次
month〔mʌnθ〕*n.* 月　　***or so*** 大約；左右
How about…? …如何？　　time〔taɪm〕*n.* 次數
week〔wik〕*n.* 週　　last〔læst〕*adj.* 過去的（= *past*）
wow〔waʊ〕*interj.* （表示驚訝、喜悅、痛苦等）哇
good〔gʊd〕*adj.* 忠實的；好的　　customer〔'kʌstəmɚ〕*n.* 顧客
owner〔'onɚ〕*n.* 物主；業主　　love〔lʌv〕*v.* 愛
sometimes〔'sʌm,taɪmz〕*adv.* 有時候；偶爾
seldom〔'sɛldəm〕*adv.* 很少

15. (**A**) Question：Where are they?

問：他們在哪裡？

M：Hi, Mary. Mind if I join you?

男：嗨，瑪麗。介意我跟妳一起嗎？

W：Not at all, Bill. Please sit down. What are you having for lunch? I'm having pizza.

女：完全不會，比爾。請坐。你午餐吃什麼？我要吃披薩。

M：I don't like pizza. I like fruit and vegetables.

男：我不喜歡披薩。我喜歡水果和蔬菜。

W：That's very healthy. Maybe I should try it.

女：那很健康。或許我應該試看看。

A. In a cafeteria. <u>在自助餐廳。</u>

B. In a library. 在圖書館。

C. In a classroom. 在教室。

* Mary ('mɛrɪ) *n.* 瑪麗   mind (maɪnd) *v.* 介意
  join (dʒɔɪn) *v.* 加入；和…一起做同樣的事
  not at all 一點也不   Bill (bɪl) *n.* 比爾   have (hæv) *v.* 吃
  lunch (lʌntʃ) *n.* 午餐   pizza ('pitsə) *n.* 披薩
  like (laɪk) *v.* 喜歡   fruit (frut) *n.* 水果
  vegetable ('vɛdʒətəbl) *n.* 蔬菜   healthy ('hɛlθɪ) *adj.* 健康的
  maybe ('mebɪ) *adv.* 或許；可能   try (traɪ) *v.* 嘗試
  cafeteria (,kæfə'tɪrɪə) *n.* 自助餐廳   library ('laɪ,brɛrɪ) *n.* 圖書館
  classroom ('klæs,rum) *n.* 教室

16. (**B**) Question : Will there be a game today?

問：今天會有比賽嗎？

W：Did you get the email I sent you yesterday?

女：你有收到我昨天寄給你的電子郵件嗎？

M：No, I haven't been able to use the Internet all week. What's up?

男：沒有，我整週都一直無法使用網路。發生什麼事？

W：The game was cancelled. We can't play today because three people are sick.

女：比賽取消了。我們今天沒辦法比賽，因爲有三個人生病了。

M：That's OK. Maybe we can play sometime next month.

男：沒關係。或許我們可以下個月找個時間比賽。

A. Yes, there will. 是的，會有。

B. No, there won't. 不，不會有。

C. Sometimes there is. 有時候會有。

* game〔gem〕*n.* 比賽　　email〔ˈiˌmel〕*n.* 電子郵件
sent〔sɛnt〕*v.* 送；寄【send 的過去式】　　able〔ˈebl〕*adj.* 能夠…的
be able to V. 能夠~　　use〔juz〕*v.* 使用
Internet〔ˈɪntəˌnɛt〕*n.* 網際網路　　**What's up?** 發生什麼事？
cancel〔ˈkænsl〕*v.* 取消　　play〔ple〕*v.* 進行比賽
today〔təˈde〕*adv.* 今天　　sick〔sɪk〕*adj.* 生病的
That's OK. 沒關係。　　sometime〔ˈsʌmˌtaɪm〕*adv.* 某時
next month 下個月　　**there be** 有

17. (**B**) Question : Does the woman know Jack Forrest?

問：女士認識傑克・福里斯特嗎？

M：Do you know Jack Forrest?

男：妳認識傑克・福里斯特嗎？

W：Yes. I've known Jack and his sister, Ann, for years.

女：認識啊。我認識傑克跟他妹妹安好幾年了。

M：I heard that Jack got into Harvard University.

男：我聽說傑克進入哈佛大學了。

W：That's no surprise. He's such a good student.

女：不意外啊。他是非常優秀的學生。

A. Yes, because she is Jack's sister.

認識，因為她是傑克的妹妹。

B. Yes, she knows him very well. 認識，她跟他非常熟。

C. No, but she knows Jack's sister.

不認識，但她認識傑克的妹妹。

* Jack Forrest〔dʒæk ˈfɔrɪst〕*n.* 傑克・福里斯特
know〔no〕*v.* 認識；知道　　sister〔ˈsɪstɚ〕*n.* 姐妹
Ann〔æn〕*n.* 安　　**for years** 很多年了；很久了

get into 進入（大學）
Harvard University〔'hɑrvəd ,junə'vɝsətɪ〕 *n.* 哈佛大學
That's no surprise. 不意外啊。　　*know sb. very well* 和某人很熟

18. (**B**) Question : What did the woman borrow?

問：女士借了什麼？

W : Can I borrow your calculator?

女：我可以跟你借計算機嗎？

M : Sure. Here you go.

男：當然。拿去吧。

W : I'll bring it right back.

女：我會馬上還給你。

M : Take your time.

男：慢慢來。

A. A computer. 電腦。
B. A calculator. <u>計算機。</u>
C. A pencil. 鉛筆。

* borrow〔'bɔro〕 *v.* 借（入）　　calculator〔'kælkjə,letə〕 *n.* 計算機
Here you go. 你要的東西在這裡；拿去吧。　　bring〔brɪŋ〕 *v.* 帶
bring sth. back 把某物拿回來　　right〔raɪt〕 *adv.* 立刻；馬上
take one's time 慢慢來；不急　　computer〔kəm'pjutə〕 *n.* 電腦

19. (**C**) Question : What color shirt does the man want?

問：男士要什麼顏色的襯衫？

M : Do you have this shirt in a different color?

男：這件襯衫你們有不同的顏色嗎？

W : It comes in black, white, gray, and blue. But we may not have every color in your size.

女：這有黑色、白色、灰色，和藍色。但你的尺寸我們可能沒有所有的顏色。

M : I'm interested in blue, size extra large.

男：我對藍色有興趣，特大號。

W : Just give me a minute and I'll look.

女：給我一分鐘，我來找看看。

A. Black. 黑色。

B. White. 白色。

C. Blue. 藍色。

* color〔'kʌlɚ〕*n.* 顏色　　shirt〔ʃɝt〕*n.* 襯衫
different〔'dɪfərənt〕*adj.* 不同的　　***come in*** 有～（顏色或尺寸）
gray〔gre〕*adj.* 灰色的　　blue〔blu〕*adj.* 藍色的
size〔saɪz〕*n.* 尺寸　　***in one's size*** 某人的尺寸
be interested in 對⋯有興趣　　extra〔'ɛkstrə〕*adv.* 額外地；特別地
large〔lɑrdʒ〕*adj.* 大的　　minute〔'mɪnɪt〕*n.* 分鐘；瞬間
look〔luk〕*v.* 看；尋找

20. (**A**) Question : Will the man go hiking tomorrow?

問：男士明天會去遠足嗎？

W : We're going on a hike in Danshui tomorrow. Would you like to come?

女：我們明天要去淡水遠足。你想要來嗎？

M : Maybe. How many people are going?

男：或許吧。有幾個人要去？

W : There should be about five of us—six if you will join us.

女：我們應該會有五個人左右——如果你願意加入我們，就六個人。

M : Sure, I'd love to go. But if it's raining, I won't come.

男：好啊，我很樂意。但如果下雨的話，我就不會去了。

A. Yes, if it is not raining. 會，如果沒有下雨的話。

B. No, definitely not. 不會，絕對不會。

C. No, because he does not like hiking.

　　不會，因為他不喜歡遠足。

* hike〔haɪk〕*v. n.* 健行；遠足　　***go on a hike*** 去健行；去遠足
about〔ə'baʊt〕*prep.* 大約　　will〔wɪl〕*aux.* 願意
would love to V. 樂意～　　rain〔ren〕*v.* 下雨
definitely〔'dɛfənɪtlɪ〕*adv.* 絕對　　because〔bɪ'kɔz〕*conj.* 因為

TEST 9 詳解

聽力：是非題

1. (**Y**) Julie is roller-skating.

茉莉在溜冰。

* roller (ˈrollɚ) *n.* 滾動的東西　　skate (sket) *v.* 滑冰；溜冰
roller-skate (ˈrolɚ͵sket) *v.* 穿輪式溜冰鞋溜冰

2. (**Y**) They are enjoying a big meal.

他們正在享受大餐。

* enjoy (ɪnˈdʒɔɪ) *v.* 享受　　meal (mil) *n.* 一餐

3. (**Y**) Ms. Foster is shopping for food.

佛斯特女士正在買食物。

* Foster〔ˈfɔstɚ〕*n.* 佛斯特　　shop〔ʃɑp〕*v.* 逛街；購物
  shop for 逛街購買　　food〔fud〕*n.* 食物

4. (**N**) This is a birthday cake.

這是一塊生日蛋糕。

* birthday〔ˈbɝθˌde〕*n.* 生日　　cake〔kek〕*n.* 蛋糕

5. (**N**) This is a library.

　　這是一家圖書館。

　　　* library ('laɪ,brɛrɪ) n. 圖書館

6. (**Y**) Jim is watching a movie.

　　吉姆正在看電影。

　　　* watch (wɑtʃ) v. 觀賞　　movie ('muvɪ) n. 電影

7. (**N**) The picture was taken in 2011.

照片是在 2011 年拍攝的。

* picture〔'pɪktʃɚ〕 *n.* 照片　　***take a picture*** 拍相

8. (**Y**) John likes bowling.

約翰喜歡打保齡球。

* bowling〔'bolɪŋ〕 *n.* 保齡球遊戲

9. (Y) The beds are unmade.

床還沒整理好。

* bed〔bɛd〕n. 床　　unmade〔ʌn'med〕adj. 尚未做好的
  make a bed 整理床鋪；鋪床

10. (Y) It is raining.

現在正在下雨。

* rain〔ren〕v. 下雨

聽力：選擇題

11. (**A**) Question : What are they doing?

問：他們正在做什麼？

W : Can I help you clean up, Bill?

女：我可以幫你打掃嗎，比爾？

M : Thanks, Annie. I really need your help. Look at the mess!

男：謝謝，安妮。真的需要妳的幫忙。看看那一團亂！

W : With the two of us, we'll have it cleaned up in no time.

女：有我們兩個，我們很快就會打掃乾淨。

M : I'll go get some extra large trash bags.

男：我去拿些特大的垃圾袋。

A. Cleaning.　打掃。

B. Planning a party.　計畫一場派對。

C. Having a party.　舉行派對。

* help〔hɛlp〕v. n. 幫助　 ***clean up*** 打掃乾淨；收拾；整理
　really〔'riəlɪ〕adv. 真的　　need〔nid〕v. 需要
　look at 看　 mess〔mɛs〕n. 一團糟；混亂的狀態
　have〔hæv〕v. 使　 ***in no time*** 很快；立刻
　extra〔'ɛkstrə〕adv. 特別地　 large〔lɑrdʒ〕adj. 大的
　trash〔træʃ〕n. 垃圾　 bag〔bæg〕n. 袋子
　plan〔plæn〕v. 計劃　 ***have a party*** 舉辦派對

12. (**A**) Question : What is Tom doing?

問：湯姆正在做什麼？

M : Hi, honey. How's Tom doing? Is he sleeping already?

男：嗨，親愛的。湯姆好嗎？他已經睡了嗎？

W : Yes, but I think he was feeling better this afternoon. He had two bottles of milk in the morning, and two more before he went to bed.

女：對，但我想今天下午他就覺得比較好了。他早上喝了兩瓶牛奶，在他去睡覺前又喝了兩瓶。

M : Oh good. At least his appetite is back. What did the
doctor say?

男：喔，很好。至少他的食慾恢復了。醫生怎麼說？

W : It's just a cold. Nothing to worry about, dear. So how
was your day at work?

女：只是感冒。沒有什麼好擔心的，親愛的。那你今天工作如何？

A. Sleeping. 睡覺。

B. Eating. 吃東西。

C. Reading. 閱讀。

* honey〔'hʌnɪ〕*n.*（常用於稱呼）親愛的
  How's sb. doing? ～好嗎？   sleep〔slip〕*v.* 睡覺
  already〔ɔl'rɛdɪ〕*adv.* 已經   think〔θɪŋk〕*v.* 想
  feel〔fil〕*v.* 感覺   bottle〔'batḷ〕*n.* 一瓶
  milk〔mɪlk〕*n.* 牛奶   ***at least*** 至少
  appetite〔'æpə,taɪt〕*n.* 食慾；胃口
  back〔bæk〕*adj.* 恢復（原狀）   doctor〔'daktɚ〕*n.* 醫生
  say〔se〕*v.* 說   cold〔kold〕*n.* 感冒
  nothing〔'nʌθɪŋ〕*n.* 沒什麼   ***worry about*** 擔心
  dear〔dɪr〕*n.*（常作稱呼）親愛的   ***at work*** 在工作
  eat〔it〕*v.* 吃   read〔rid〕*v.* 閱讀

13. (**B**) Question : What is the girl doing?

問：女孩正在做什麼？

W : Atlantic, Pacific, Indian, Arctic…

女：大西洋、太平洋、印度洋、北極海…

M : Helen, what are you doing?

男：海倫，妳在做什麼？

W : I'm preparing for my geography test tomorrow. I was
listing the names of all the oceans. By the way, do you
know which continent Russia belongs to?

女：我正在為我明天的地理考試做準備。我正列出所有大洋的名
字。對了，你知道俄羅斯是屬於哪一洲嗎？

M：Is Russia part of Europe or Asia? To be honest, I'm not
   sure.

男：俄羅斯是歐洲還是亞洲的一部份？老實說，我不確定。

A. Planning a trip. 計畫旅行。

B. Studying for a test. 為考試而唸書。

C. Going abroad. 出國。

* Atlantic〔ət'læntɪk〕*n.* 大西洋   Pacific〔pə'sɪfɪk〕*n.* 太平洋
  Indian〔'ɪndɪən〕*n.* 印度洋   Arctic〔'ɑrktɪk〕*n.* 北極地帶；北極海
  prepare〔prɪ'pɛr〕*v.* 準備 *< for >*
  geography〔dʒɪ'ɑgrəfɪ〕*n.* 地理學   test〔tɛst〕*n.* 測驗；小考
  list〔lɪst〕*v.* 列出   name〔nem〕*n.* 名字
  ocean〔'oʃən〕*n.* 海洋   ***by the way*** 順便一提
  continent〔'kɑntənənt〕*n.* 洲；大陸   Russia〔'rʌʃə〕*n.* 俄羅斯
  belong to 屬於   ***be (a) part of*** 是⋯的一部份
  Europe〔'jurəp〕*n.* 歐洲   Asia〔'eʃə〕*n.* 亞洲
  honest〔'ɑnɪst〕*adj.* 誠實的   ***to be honest*** 老實說
  sure〔ʃur〕*adj.* 確定的   plan〔plæn〕*v.* 計畫；打算
  trip〔trɪp〕*n.* 旅行   study〔'stʌdɪ〕*v.* 讀書
  abroad〔ə'brɔd〕*adv.* 在國外；到國外   ***go abroad*** 出國

14. (**C**) Question：What does the woman like to read about?
     問：這女士喜歡閱讀什麼？

     M：Do you read comic books?

     男：妳看漫畫書嗎？

     W：Sometimes. If there's nothing else to read.

     女：有時候。如果沒有其他東西好讀的時候。

     M：Then what do you like to read?

     男：那妳喜歡讀什麼？

     W：I like non-fiction books, like history and science.

     女：我喜歡非小說類的書，像是歷史和科學。

     A. Comics. 漫畫。

     B. Novels. 小說。

     C. History and science. 歷史和科學。

* ***comic books*** 漫畫書（＝*comics*）
sometimes〔'sʌm,taɪmz〕*adv.* 有時候；偶爾
else〔pæs〕*adj.* 其他的
non-fiction〔nɑn'fɪkʃən〕*adj.* 非小說類的
history〔'hɪstərɪ〕*n.* 歷史   science〔'saɪəns〕*n.* 科學；自然科學
novel〔'nɑvḷ〕*n.* 小說

15. (**C**) Question：What are they talking about?
   問：他們在談論什麼？

   W：Who is planning the Christmas party?
   女：誰正在計畫這次的聖誕派對？

   M：Tina is planning the party. Why?
   男：蒂娜正在計畫派對。爲什麼怎麼問？

   W：I just wonder what she has planned.
   女：我只是好奇她計畫了什麼。

   M：I'm sure Tina has some fun activities for us. She always
      does.
   男：我確定蒂娜爲我們準備了有趣的活動。她總是這麼做。

   A. Their teacher. 他們的老師。
   B. Their homework. 他們的家庭作業。
   C. A Christmas party. 聖誕派對。

   * ***talk about*** 談論   Christmas〔'krɪsməs〕*n.* 聖誕節
   party〔'pɑrtɪ〕*n.* 派對   wonder〔'wʌndə〕*v.* 想知道
   fun〔fʌn〕*adj.* 有趣的   activity〔æk'tɪvətɪ〕*n.* 活動
   always〔'ɔlwez〕*adv.* 總是   homework〔'hom,wɝk〕*n.* 家庭作業

16. (**A**) Question：Who is the woman?
   問：這女士是誰？

   M：I'd like to speak with the boss.
   男：我想要跟老闆說話。

   W：I am the boss.
   女：我是老闆。

M : You!? You're young enough to be my daughter.

男：妳 !? 妳夠年輕可以當我女兒了。

W : But I'm still the boss. How can I help you, sir?

女：但是我仍然還是老板。我能幫您什麼嗎，先生？

A. The boss. 老闆。

B. A customer. 顧客。

C. The man's daughter. 男士的女兒。

* speak〔spik〕v. 說話　　boss〔bɔs〕n. 老板
　young〔jʌŋ〕adj. 年輕的　　enough〔ə'nʌf〕adv. 足夠地
　daughter〔'dɔtə〕n. 女兒　　still〔stɪl〕adv. 仍然
　sir〔sɝ〕n. 先生　　customer〔'kʌstəmə〕n. 顧客

17. (**C**) Question : Did the man give the woman her change?

　　問：男士有把找的錢給女士嗎？

W : Did you give me my change?

女：你有找錢給我嗎？

M : Yes, I did. I gave it to you with the bag.

男：是的，我有。我連同那個袋子一併交給您。

W : Oh, here it is. I put it in the bag. My mistake.

女：喔，在這裡。我放進袋子裡。是我的錯。

M : That's OK. Have a nice day.

男：沒關係。祝您有美好的一天。

A. No, the man forgot to give the woman her change.

　　沒有，男士忘記找女士錢。

B. No. The woman does not need any change.

　　沒有，女士不需要任何零錢。

C. Yes, the man gave her the change. 有，男士有找錢給她。

* give〔gɪv〕v. 給　　change〔tʃendʒ〕n. 零錢；找零
　mistake〔mɪ'stek〕n. 錯誤　　***That's OK.*** 沒關係。
　Have a nice day. 祝您有美好的一天。
　forgot〔fə'gɑt〕v. 忘記【forget 的過去式】

18. (**B**) Question : What is expensive in New York?

問：什麼在紐約很昂貴？

M : New York is the most popular city with tourists.

男：紐約是最受觀光客歡迎的城市。

W : I've heard people say it's very expensive to travel there.

女：我聽人們說過去那裡旅遊非常昂貴。

M : Hotel prices are very high. I'm not sure about everything else.

男：飯店價格非常高。我不確定其他事物的價錢。

W : If I ever go there, I'll remember to bring plenty of money.

女：如果我到那裡，我會記得要帶一大筆錢。

A. Taxis. 計程車。

B. Hotels. 飯店。

C. Food. 食物。

* expensive (ɪk'spɛnsɪv) *adj.* 昂貴的　　New York (nju'jɔrk) *n.* 紐約
popular ('pɑpjələ) *adj.* 受歡迎的　　tourist ('tʊrɪst) *n.* 觀光客
hear (hɪr) *v.* 聽到　　travel ('trævl̩) *v.* 旅行
hotel (ho'tɛl) *n.* 旅館；飯店　　price (praɪs) *n.* 價格
high (haɪ) *adj.* 高的　　sure (ʃur) *adj.* 確定的
everything ('ɛvrɪˌθɪŋ) *pron.* 一切事物　　else (ɛls) *adj.* 其他的
remember (rɪ'mɛmbə) *v.* 記得　　bring (brɪŋ) *v.* 帶
plenty of 大量的　　taxi ('tɛksɪ) *n.* 計程車

19. (**B**) Question : Will the woman study tonight?

問：女士今晚會唸書嗎？

W : I'm too tired to study tonight.

女：今晚我太累，以致於無法讀書。

M : But don't you have a big exam tomorrow?

男：但是妳明天不是有一個大考嗎？

W : Yes, but I've studied as much as I can. I need a break.

女：對，但我已經盡可能地努力唸書了。我需要休息。

M：That's probably a good idea. I always do better on
　　exams when I've had a good night's rest.

男：那或許是個好主意。當我一夜好眠時，我考試總是考得比較好。

A. Yes, she will. 是的，她會。

B. No, she won't. 不，她不會。

C. Maybe, she did. 或許，她唸過。

* ***too…to~*** 太…以致於不~ 　　　tired〔taɪrd〕*adj.* 疲倦的；累的
exam〔ɪgˋzæm〕*n.* 考試　　***as much as sb. can*** 盡可能
break〔brek〕*n.* 休息　　probably〔ˋprɑbəblɪ〕*adv.* 可能
do better 考得比較好　　idea〔aɪˋdiə〕*n.* 主意　　rest〔rɛst〕*n.* 休息

20. (**A**) Question：Where did the conversation take place?

問：這段對話是在哪裡發生的？

M：Did you see that?

男：妳有看到那個嗎？

W：I sure did. That guy just drove through the red light.

女：我當然有。那個傢伙剛剛闖紅燈。

M：That's so dangerous. He could have killed someone.

男：那真的很危險。他可能會害人喪命。

W：He was lucky there isn't much traffic at this hour.

女：他很幸運，這個時間沒有什麼車。

A. On the street. 在街上。

B. In a library. 在圖書館裡。

C. On an airplane. 在飛機上。

* guy〔gaɪ〕*n.* 人；傢伙　　ran〔ræn〕*v.* 衝過【run 的過去式】
light〔laɪt〕*n.* 燈
drive through the red light 闖紅燈（= *run a red light*）
dangerous〔ˋdendʒərəs〕*adj.* 危險的
kill〔kɪl〕*v.* 殺死　　lucky〔ˋlʌkɪ〕*adj.* 幸運的
traffic〔ˋtræfɪk〕*n.* 交通；交通流量；（來往的）行人、車輛
hour〔aur〕*n.* 時刻；時間　　conversation〔͵kɑnvɚˋseʃən〕*n.* 談話
take place 發生　　airplane〔ˋɛr͵plen〕*n.* 飛機

TEST 10 詳解

聽力：是非題

1. (**N**) Jane eats a lot of fast food.
　　　　珍吃很多速食。

　　　* *a lot of* 很多　　*fast food* 速食

2. (**Y**) Timmy is wearing sunglasses.
　　　　提米戴著太陽眼鏡。

　　　* Timmy〔'tɪmɪ〕*n.* 提米　　wear〔wɛr〕*v.* 穿；戴
　　　sunglasses〔'sʌn,glæsɪz〕*n. pl.* 太陽眼鏡

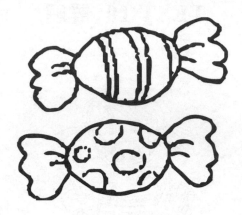

3. (**N**) There are three pieces of candy.

有三顆糖果。

* ***there + be*** 有～　　piece〔pis〕*n.* 塊；顆

　candy〔'kændɪ〕*n.* 糖果

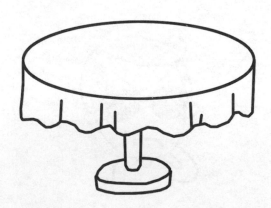

4. (**Y**) The table is covered with a cloth.

這桌子被桌布覆蓋著。

* table〔'tebḷ〕*n.* 桌子　　cover〔'kʌvɚ〕*v.* 覆蓋

　be covered with 被…覆蓋　　cloth〔klɔθ〕*n.* 布；桌布

5. (**N**) Mike is hunting.

麥克在打獵。

 * hunt〔hʌnt〕v. 打獵

6. (**N**) Tom is planting a tree.

湯姆正在種樹。

 * plant〔plænt〕v. 種植　　tree〔tri〕n. 樹

7. (**Y**) It is time for lunch.

　　　　該是吃午餐的時候了。

　　　　*　It's time for*…　該是…的時候了。　　　lunch〔 lʌntʃ 〕 *n.* 午餐

8. (**N**) The girls are standing still.

　　　　女孩們站著不動。

　　　　*　stand〔 stænd 〕*v.* 站　　　still〔 stɪl 〕*adj.* 不動的

9. (**Y**) Food and drinks are not allowed.

不可飲食。

* food〔fud〕*n.* 食物　　drink〔drɪŋk〕*n.* 飲料
allow〔ə'laʊ〕*v.* 允許

10. (**Y**) The mother is holding a child.

媽媽正抱著小孩。

* hold〔hold〕*v.* 握著；抱著　　child〔tʃaɪld〕*n.* 小孩

聽力：選擇題

11. (**B**) Question : Why is the woman in a hurry?

　　　　問：為何女士很匆忙？

　　　　M : What's the hurry?

　　　　男：在急什麼？

　　　　W : I'm late for class.

　　　　女：我上課遲到了。

　　　　M : Do you need a ride? I can drive you to school.

　　　　男：需要我載妳嗎？我可以載妳到學校。

　　　　W : That would be great.

　　　　女：那真是太棒了。

　　　　A. She's late for work. 她上班遲到了。

　　　　B. She's late for school. <u>她上學遲到了。</u>

　　　　C. She's late for a party. 她派對遲到了。

　　　　* hurry (ˈhɝɪ) *n.* 匆忙　　***in a hurry*** 匆忙的
　　　　What's the hurry? 在急什麼？　　late (let) *adj.* 遲到的
　　　　class (klæs) *n.* 上課　　ride (raɪd) *n.* 搭乘；乘車
　　　　drive (draɪv) *v.* 開車載 (某人)　　great (gret) *adj.* 很棒的
　　　　work (wɝk) *n.* 工作　　party (ˈpɑrtɪ) *n.* 派對

12. (**B**) Question : What day is it?

　　　　問：今天星期幾？

　　　　W : Where did your sister go?

　　　　女：妳妹妹去了哪裡？

　　　　M : She went to meet her friends at the library. They meet
　　　　　　 for a study group every Saturday.

　　　　男：她去圖書館和她的朋友見面。他們每週六都因為讀書會見面。

　　　　W : What subject do they study?

　　　　女：他們讀什麼科目？

　　　　M : They study science and history.

　　　　男：他們讀科學和歷史。

A. Friday. 星期五。

B. Saturday. 星期六。

C. Sunday. 星期日。

* went〔wɛnt〕v. 去【go 的過去式】　meet〔mit〕v. 和～見面
　friend〔frɛnd〕n. 朋友　library〔'laɪˌbrɛrɪ〕n. 圖書館
　study〔'stʌdɪ〕n. 讀書　group〔grup〕n. 群；組
　study group 讀書會　subject〔'sʌbdʒɪkt〕n. 科目
　science〔'saɪəns〕n. 科學　history〔'hɪstrɪ〕n. 歷史

13. (**B**) Question : When will the woman arrive at the bus station?

問：女士何時會到達公車站？

M : Call me when you arrive at the bus station. I'll come pick you up.

男：當妳到公車站時，打電話給我。我會去接妳。

W : You don't have to do that, Sam. I won't be there until after midnight. It's too late.

女：你不需要那樣做，山姆。我要午夜後才會到那裡。那太晚了。

M : No problem. I don't mind at all. It will be difficult to find a taxi at that hour.

男：沒關係。我完全不介意。那時候很難找到計程車。

W : If you insist.

女：如果你堅持的話。

A. Before sunset. 在日落前。

B. After midnight. 在午夜後。

C. Noon. 中午。

* arrive〔ə'raɪv〕v. 到達　bus〔bʌs〕n. 公車
　station〔'steʃən〕n. 車站　call〔kɔl〕v. 打電話給（某人）
　pick sb. **up** 開車接某人　**have to** V. 必須～
　not…until～ 直到～才…
　midnight〔'mɪdˌnaɪt〕n. 午夜【晚上十二點】
　late〔let〕adj. 晚的　**No problem.** 沒關係；不麻煩。
　mind〔maɪnd〕v. 介意　**not…at all** 一點也不…
　difficult〔'dɪfəˌkʌlt〕adj. 困難的　taxi〔'tæksɪ〕n. 計程車

hour〔aur〕*n.* 小時;時刻　　insist〔ɪn'sɪst〕*v.* 堅持
If you insist. 如果你堅持的話;如果你一定要這樣的話。
sunset〔'sʌn,sɛt〕*n.* 日落　　noon〔nun〕*n.* 中午

14. (**A**) Question : What does the man think the woman should wear?

問:男士認為女士應該穿什麼?

W : Which looks better on me, the short dress or the long
skirt?

女:哪一件我穿起來比較好看,短洋裝還是長裙?

M : They both look good on you.

男:你兩件穿起來都好看。

W : Come on! Make a choice.

女:快點!做個選擇。

M : Well, it's pretty hot outside, so you'll probably be more
comfortable in the short dress.

男:嗯,外面非常熱,所以你可能穿短洋裝比較舒服。

A. The short dress. 短洋裝。

B. The long skirt. 長裙。

C. Jeans. 牛仔褲。

* look〔luk〕*v.* 看起來　　***look good on*** sb. 穿在某人身上很好看
short〔ʃɔrt〕*adj.* 短的　　dress〔drɛs〕*n.* 洋裝
long〔lɔŋ〕*adj.* 長的　　skirt〔skɝt〕*n.* 裙子
Come on! 來吧;快點!　　choice〔tʃɔɪs〕*n.* 選擇
make a choice 做選擇　　well〔wɛl〕*interj.*（表示停頓、遲疑）嗯
outside〔'aut'said〕*adv.* 在外面　　pretty〔'prɪtɪ〕*adv.* 非常
hot〔hɑt〕*adj.* 熱的　　probably〔'prɑbəblɪ〕*adv.* 可能
comfortable〔'kʌmfətəbļ〕*adj.* 舒服的　　in〔ɪn〕*prep.* 穿著
jeans〔dʒinz〕*n.* 牛仔褲

15. (**C**) Question : Is Peter tall?

問:彼得很高嗎?

M : Where did you meet your friend Peter?

男:妳在哪裡認識你的朋友彼得的?

W : We met in school. He was in my math class and sat in the row behind me.

女：我們在學校認識的。他和我一起上數學課，坐在我的後排。

M : He's very tall. I was surprised to know that he was our age.

男：他很高。當我知道他跟我們同年時，我很驚訝。

W : Yes, he's almost 190 centimeters.

女：是的，他將近 190 公分。

A. No, he isn't. 不，他不高。

B. Sometimes, he will. 有時候他會。

C. Yes, he is. 是的，他很高。

* Peter〔'pitɚ〕*n.* 彼得　　tall〔tɔl〕*adj.* 高的　　meet〔mit〕*v.* 認識
math〔mæθ〕*n.* 數學　　class〔klæs〕*n.* 課
row〔ro〕*n.* 一排座位　　behind〔bɪ'haɪnd〕*prep.* 在…後面
surprised〔sə'praɪzd〕*adj.* 驚訝的　　age〔edʒ〕*n.* 年紀
almost〔'ɔl,most〕*adv.* 幾乎；將近
centimeter〔'sɛntə,mitɚ〕*n.* 公分
sometimes〔'sʌm,taɪmz〕*adv.* 有時候；偶爾

16. (**C**) Question : What did the girl do?

問：女孩做了什麼？

W : I've finished all my homework. Can I watch TV now?

女：我已經做完我所有的功課。現在我可以看電視嗎？

M : Sure, but don't stay up too late.

男：當然，但是別熬夜到太晚。

W : I know. I won't stay up too late, I promise.

女：我知道。我不會熬夜到太晚，我保證。

M : Good.

男：很好。

A. She turned on the radio. 她打開收音機。

B. She went to bed. 她上床睡覺。

C. She finished her homework. 她做完她的功課。

* finish〔'fɪnɪʃ〕v. 完成　　homework〔'hom,wɝk〕n. 功課
watch TV 看電視　　sure〔ʃur〕adv. 當然
stay up 熬夜　　promise〔'pramɪs〕v. 保證；答應
turn on 打開（電器）　　radio〔'redɪ,o〕n. 收音機
go to bed 上床睡覺

17.(**B**) Question : Who has been to Japan?

問：誰去過日本？

M：My family is going to Japan this summer.　I'm really excited.　I've never been there.

男：我們家今年夏天要去日本。我真的很興奮。我從來沒去過。

W：You'll love it!　There's so much to see and do.　And the countryside is very beautiful.

女：你會愛上日本！有很多東西可以看，和很多事可以做。而且鄉村很美麗。

M：What are the people like?

男：那裡的人怎麼樣？

W：They're kind of quiet, but very polite and friendly.

女：他們有點安靜，但是非常有禮貌和友善。

A. The man. 男士。

B. The woman. 女士。

C. Both the man and the woman. 男士和女士都去過。

* Japan〔dʒə'pæn〕n. 日本　　family〔'fæməlɪ〕n. 家庭
summer〔'sʌmɚ〕n. 夏天　　excited〔ɪk'saɪtɪd〕adj. 興奮的
have been to 去過~　　countryside〔'kʌntrɪ,saɪd〕n. 鄉村
beautiful〔'bjutəfəl〕adj. 美麗的
What are the people like? 那裡的人如何？
kind of 有點（ = a little）　　quiet〔'kwaɪət〕adj. 安靜的
polite〔pə'laɪt〕adj. 有禮貌的
friendly〔'frɛndlɪ〕adj. 友善的

18.(**B**) Question : Where are they?

問：他們在哪裡？

W : Oh, no! We missed the last train.

女：喔，不！我們錯過最後一班火車了。

M : I guess we'll have to walk home. Are the buses still running?

男：我想我們必須走路回家。公車還有開嗎？

W : I think so, but the buses aren't safe at night. I'd rather pay for a taxi.

女：我想有，但是晚上公車不安全。我寧願花錢坐計程車。

M : That's fine with me.

男：我沒問題。

A. On a bus. 在公車上。
B. At the train station. 在火車站。
C. At home. 在家。

* miss〔mɪs〕v. 錯過　　last〔læst〕adj. 最後的
  train〔tren〕n. 火車　　guess〔gɛs〕v. 猜想；認為
  walk〔wɔk〕v. 走路　　still〔stɪl〕adv. 仍然
  run〔rʌn〕v. 運作；行駛　　safe〔sef〕adj. 安全的
  would rather V. 寧願～　　**pay for** 為…付錢；支付…的錢
  That's fine with me. 我沒問題；我不介意。
  train station 火車站

19. (**A**) Question : What happened last night?

問：昨晚發生了什麼事？

M : Hi, Mary. Sorry I didn't call you last night. We had an emergency.

男：嗨，瑪麗。很抱歉我昨晚沒有打電話給妳。我們有緊急事故。

W : What happened, John?

女：發生什麼事了，約翰？

M : My daughter got very sick, so we took her to the hospital.

男：我女兒病得很嚴重，所以我們帶她去醫院。

W : That's awful. I hope she's OK.

女：那真糟糕。我希望她沒事。

A. The man took his daughter to the hospital.
　　男士帶他的女兒去醫院。

B. The woman's son got very ill. 女士的兒子病得很重。

C. The man called the woman. 男士打電話給女士。

* happen〔ˈhæpən〕v. 發生　　call〔kɔl〕v. 打電話給（某人）
　emergency〔ɪˈmɛdʒənsɪ〕n. 緊急情況
　daughter〔ˈdɔtɚ〕n. 女兒
　got〔gɑt〕v. 變得【get 的過去式】　　sick〔sɪk〕adj. 生病的
　hospital〔ˈhɑspɪtḷ〕n. 醫院　　awful〔ˈɔfʊl〕adj. 糟糕的；嚴重的
　hope〔hop〕v. 希望　　son〔sʌn〕n. 兒子

20. (**C**) Question：Will the woman buy milk at the market?
　　　　問：女士會在市場買牛奶嗎？

W：I'm going to the market. What do we need?

女：我要去市場。我們需要什麼嗎？

M：We're out of milk and butter.

男：我們牛奶和奶油沒了。

W：Right. How about coffee?

女：沒錯。咖啡呢？

M：I have plenty. But we're running low on sugar.

男：我有很多。但是我們的糖要用完了。

A. No. She will buy coffee. 不會。她會買咖啡。

B. She will not go to the market. 她不會去市場。

C. Yes, she will. 是的，她會。

* buy〔baɪ〕v. 買　　milk〔mɪlk〕n. 牛奶
　market〔ˈmɑrkɪt〕n. 市場　　need〔nid〕v. 需要
　out of 沒有　　butter〔ˈbʌtɚ〕n. 奶油
　right〔raɪt〕adj. 對的　　*How about~?* 如何～？
　coffee〔ˈkɔfɪ〕n. 咖啡
　plenty〔ˈplɛntɪ〕n. 豐富；多量　　low〔lo〕adj. 短缺的
　run low on sth. 某物快用完了　　sugar〔ˈʃʊgɚ〕n. 糖

TEST 11 詳解

聽力:是非題

1. (**Y**) The snowman is wearing a scarf.

   雪人正戴著圍巾。

   * snowman ('sno,mæn) *n.* 雪人　　wear (wɛr) *v.* 穿;戴
     scarf (skɑrf) *n.* 圍巾

2. (**Y**) Helen will eat the ice cream.

   海倫會吃了冰淇淋。

   * Helen ('hɛlən) *n.* 海倫　　eat (it) *v.* 吃
     ice cream ('aɪs'krim) *n.* 冰淇淋

3. (**Y**) The turtle is in the water.

烏龜在水中。

* turtle 〔'tɜtḷ〕 *n.* 烏龜　　water 〔'wɔtɚ〕 *n.* 水

4. (**Y**) Gina is having trouble with her algebra.

吉娜學代數遇到困難。

* Gina 〔'dʒɪnə〕 *n.* 吉娜　　trouble 〔'trʌbḷ〕 *n.* 麻煩；困難
have trouble with 有…的困難　　algebra 〔'ældʒəbrə〕 *n.* 代數（學）

5. (**N**) There are clouds in the sky.

天空有雲。

* ***there + be*** 有~   cloud〔klaʊd〕*n.* 雲
   sky〔skaɪ〕*n.* 天空

6. (**Y**) A can of Coke costs 15 dollars.

一罐可口可樂要十五元。

* can〔kæn〕*n.* 罐子   Coke〔kok〕*n.* 可口可樂（= *Coca-Cola* ）
   cost〔kɔst〕*v.*（事物）花費   dollar〔'dɑlɚ〕*n.* 元

Name	Age	Food	Color	Sport
Jimmy	8	Juice	Pink	Baseball
Tom	10	Ice cream	Green	Basketball
Sandy	12	Chicken	Purple	Dodge ball
Ben	12	Pizza	Orange	Swim

7. (**Y**) Ben's favorite color is orange.

班最喜愛的顏色是橘色。

* favorite〔ˈfevərɪt〕*adj.* 最喜愛的　　　color〔ˈkɑlɚ〕*n.* 顏色
   orange〔ˈɔrɪndʒ〕*n.* 橘色

8. (**Y**) Henry enjoys swimming.

亨利喜歡游泳。

* Henry〔ˈhɛnrɪ〕*n.* 亨利　　　enjoy〔ɪnˈdʒɔɪ〕*v.* 喜歡；享受
   swim〔swɪm〕*v.* 游泳

9. (**N**) The father has three daughters.

父親有三個女兒。

* daughter〔'dɔtɚ〕*n.* 女兒

10. (**Y**) Veronica is a good singer.

薇若妮卡很會唱歌。

* Veronica〔vəˈrɑnɪkə〕*n.* 薇若妮卡　　　singer〔'sɪŋɚ〕*n.* 歌手

聽力：選擇題

11. (**C**) Question : What will cost 14,000 dollars?

問：什麼要花費一萬四千元？

M：Your total comes to 14,000 dollars.

男：妳的總額是一萬四千元。

W：14,000 dollars!? Why so much?

女：一萬四千元 !? 爲何這麼貴？

M：Well, I had to put new tires on your car and fix the brakes.

男：嗯，我必須在妳的車子裝上新輪胎和修理煞車。

W：That's still way too much. I'm going to call my husband.

女：那還是太貴了。我要打電話給我老公。

A. Calling the woman's husband. 打電話給女士的老公。

B. The woman's vacation. 女士的假期。

C. Fixing the woman's car. <u>修理女士的車。</u>

* total〔ˋtotḷ〕*n.* 總額　　***come to*** 到達；共計
well〔wɛl〕*interj.*（表示停頓、遲疑）嗯　　***have to V.*** 必須～
tire〔taɪr〕*n.* 輪胎　　fix〔fɪks〕*v.* 修理
brake〔brek〕*n.* 煞車　　still〔stɪl〕*adv.* 仍然
way〔we〕*adv.* 大大地　　call〔kɔl〕*v.* 打電話給（某人）
husband〔ˋhʌzbənd〕*n.* 丈夫；老公　　vacation〔veˋkeʃən〕*n.* 假期

12. (**C**) Question : What is Bob's problem?

問：鮑伯有什麼問題？

W：Dinner's ready, Bob! Go wash up before you sit at the table.

女：晚餐準備好了，鮑伯！在坐在飯桌前，先去洗手。

M：I'm not hungry, Mom.

男：我不餓，媽。

W：What's wrong?

女：怎麼了？

M：I have a stomachache. I feel like I'm going to throw up.

男：我胃痛。我覺得我要吐了。

A. He is bored. 他很無聊。

B. He is too busy. 他太忙碌。

C. His stomach hurts. 他胃痛。

* dinner〔'dɪnɚ〕*n.* 晚餐　　ready〔'rɛdɪ〕*adj.* 準備好的
  go wash up 去洗手（= *go to wash* = *go and wash*）
  wash up 洗手；洗臉　　table〔'tebḷ〕*n.* 桌子
  hungry〔'hʌŋgrɪ〕*adj.* 飢餓的　　***What's wrong?*** 怎麼了？
  stomachache〔'stʌməkˌek〕*n.* 胃痛　　***feel like*** 覺得好像
  throw up 嘔吐　　problem〔'prabləm〕*n.* 問題
  bored〔bord〕*adj.* 無聊的　　busy〔'bɪzɪ〕*adj.* 忙碌的
  stomach〔'stʌmək〕*n.* 胃　　hurt〔hɝt〕*v.* 疼痛

13. (**A**) Question：Where is the woman?

    問：這位女士在哪裡？

    M：Welcome back, Ms. Hopkins. Will you be sitting at your usual table?

    男：歡迎回來，霍布金斯女士。妳今天要坐在妳平常坐的位子嗎？

    W：No, I think I'd like to sit by the window tonight.

    女：不，我今晚想要坐在窗邊。

    M：Right this way. Will you be dining alone tonight, Ms. Hopkins?

    男：這裡請。妳今晚要獨自用餐嗎，霍布金斯女士？

    W：Yes, my husband is out of town this evening.

    女：是的，我老公今天傍晚出城了。

    A. At a restaurant. 在餐廳。

    B. Out of town. 出城。

    C. At the office. 在辦公室。

    * welcome〔'wɛlkəm〕*interj.* 歡迎　　Ms.〔mɪz〕*n.* 女士
      Hopkins〔'hapkɪnz〕*n.* 霍布金斯
      usual〔'juʒʊəl〕*adj.* 經常的；平常的　　by〔baɪ〕*prep.* 在…旁邊
      right〔raɪt〕*adv.* 恰好；正好　　dine〔daɪn〕*v.* 用餐

alone〔ə'lon〕*adv.* 獨自　　town〔taʊn〕*n.* 城鎮
be out of town 出城　　evening〔'ivənɪŋ〕*n.* 傍晚
restaurant〔'rɛstərənt〕*n.* 餐廳　　office〔'ɔfɪs〕*n.* 辦公室

14. (**B**) Question : Will Betty ask Mike to do something?

問：貝蒂會請求麥可做事嗎？

W : Are you busy this afternoon, Mike?

女：你今天下午忙嗎，麥克？

M : I have no plans so far.

男：我目前沒有計畫。

W : I was wondering if you could do something for me.

女：我在想你是否可能幫我做一件事。

M : Sure, anything, Betty.

男：當然，什麼事都行，貝蒂。

A. No, she won't. 不，她不會。

B. Yes, she will. 是的，她會。

C. Yes, she was. 是的，她之前是。

* plan〔plæn〕*n.* 計畫　　*so far* 到目前為止
wonder〔'wʌndə〕*v.* 想知道
I was wondering 我在想～【過去進行式表示「婉轉、禮貌」】
sure〔ʃʊr〕*adv.* 當然

15. (**C**) Question : Why didn't the woman eat the cookies?

問：為何女士沒有吃餅乾？

M : I have some chocolate chip cookies. Would you like some?

男：我有一些巧克力薄片餅乾。妳想要吃一些嗎？

W : I would love some, but I'm going to the dentist this afternoon.

女：我想要吃一些，但是我今天下午要去看牙醫。

M : Oh, I see. It's probably not a good idea to eat cookies before seeing the dentist. Do you have a toothache?

男：喔，我知道了。去看牙醫之前吃餅乾，可能不是個好主意。妳
　　牙痛嗎？

W：No, I'm just going in for my regular cleaning and checkup.

女：不是，我只是去定期清潔跟檢查。

A. She is on a diet. 她在節食。

B. She has a toothache. 她牙痛。

C. She will go to the dentist later in the day.
　　她當天稍後要去看牙醫。

* cookie (ˈkʊkɪ) *n.* 餅乾　　chocolate (ˈtʃɔkəlɪt) *n.* 巧克力
  chip (tʃɪp) *n.* 薄片　　***would like*** 想要 (= *would love*)
  dentist (ˈdɛntɪst) *n.* 牙醫　　***go to the dentist*** 去看牙醫
  I see. 我知道了。　　probably (ˈprɑbəblɪ) *adv.* 可能
  idea (aɪˈdiə) *n.* 主意　　toothache (ˈtuθ͵ek) *n.* 牙痛
  go in for 從事；參加　　regular (ˈrɛgjələ) *adj.* 定期的
  cleaning (ˈklinɪŋ) *n.* 清潔　　checkup (ˈtʃɛk͵ʌp) *n.* 檢查
  be on a diet 節食　　later (ˈletə) *adv.* 稍後

16. (**C**) Question : What is the man?

問：男士的職業是什麼？

W : What is your year and major?

女：你幾年級，主修什麼科目？

M : I'm a senior studying history.

男：我大四，主修歷史。

W : Oh, so you want to be a teacher?

女：喔，所以你想要當老師？

M : No, I'm not sure yet. Maybe I'll be a writer.

男：不，我還沒確定。或許我可能會當作家。

A. A writer. 律師。

B. A teacher. 警察。

C. A college student. 大學生。

* year (jɪr) *n.* 年級　　major (ˈmedʒə) *n.* 主修科目

senior〔'sinjɚ〕 *n.* 大四學生　　study〔'stʌdɪ〕 *v.* 研讀
history〔'hɪstrɪ〕 *n.* 歷史　　sure〔ʃʊr〕 *adj.* 確定的
not…yet 尚未；還沒　　maybe〔'mebɪ〕 *adv.* 或許；可能
writer〔'raɪtɚ〕 *n.* 作者；作家　　college〔'kɑlɪdʒ〕 *n.* 大學

17. (**A**) Question：What does the man want?

問：男士要什麼？

M：How much is this smartphone?

男：這支智慧型手機多少錢？

W：We have a special deal today.　It's free if you sign a two-year contract.

女：我們今天有特價。如果你簽下兩年的合約，手機就免費。

M：Hmm, I already have a contract.　I'm only interested in the phone.

男：嗯，我已經有個合約了。我只對手機有興趣。

W：In that case, it's 3,000 dollars.

女：那樣的話，要三千元。

A. He wants to buy a smartphone. 他想要買一支智慧型手機。

B. He wants to sell his watch. 他想要賣他的手錶。

C. He wants to sign a contract. 他想要簽合約。

* smartphone〔'smɑrt͵fon〕 *n.* 智慧型手機
special〔'spɛʃəl〕 *adj.* 特別的　　deal〔dil〕 *n.* 交易
special deal 特價　　free〔fri〕 *adj.* 免費的
sign〔saɪn〕 *v.* 簽（合約）　　contract〔'kɑntrækt〕 *n.* 合約
hmm〔hm〕 *interj.* （表示遲疑、停頓）唔；嗯
already〔ɔl'rɛdɪ〕 *adv.* 已經　　***be interested in*** 對…有興趣
in that case 那樣的話　　sell〔sɛl〕 *v.* 賣　　watch〔wɑtʃ〕 *n.* 手錶

18. (**C**) Question：Where are they?

問：他們在哪裡？

M：Are you ready to order?

男：妳準備好要點餐了嗎？

W : Yes. I'll have the pork chops with apple sauce.

女：是的。我要豬排配蘋果醬汁。

M : Anything to drink?

男：飲料呢？

W : Give me a glass of juice, please.

女：請給我一杯果汁。

A. In a bank. 在銀行。

B. In a library. 在圖書館。

C. In a restaurant. 在餐廳。

* order〔'ɔrdɚ〕v. 點菜　　pork〔pɔrk〕n. 豬肉
chop〔tʃɑp〕n. 肉片　***pork chop*** 豬排　apple〔'æpl̩〕n. 蘋果
sauce〔sɔs〕n. 醬；調味汁　　drink〔drɪŋk〕v. 喝
glass〔glæs〕n. 玻璃杯；一杯　　juice〔dʒus〕n. 果汁
bank〔bæŋk〕n. 銀行　　library〔'laɪ,brɛrɪ〕n. 圖書館

19. (**B**) Question : What is the woman looking for?

問：女士正在找什麼？

W : Excuse me. I think I got off at the wrong stop. Is this Brookfield?

女：對不起。我想我下錯站了。這是布魯克菲爾德站嗎？

M : No, it's West Riverside. Where are you trying to go?

男：不，這是西河畔站。妳要去哪裡？

W : I'm looking for the Brookfield Hospital.

女：我在找布魯克菲爾德醫院。

M : Well, you're in the right place. This is the stop for the hospital. Once you exit the station, turn right. Then follow the signs.

男：嗯，妳在對的地方。這一站會到那家醫院。妳一出這個站，就右轉。然後照著標示走。

A. Her friend. 她的朋友。

B. The hospital. 醫院。

C. A train station. 火車站。

* ***look for*** 尋找　　***Excuse me.*** 對不起；很抱歉。　　***get off*** 下車
wrong〔rɔŋ〕*adj.* 錯的　　stop〔stɑp〕*n.* 停車站
Brookfield〔'brʊk,fild〕*n.* 布魯克菲爾德【位於美國威斯康辛州】
west〔wɛst〕*adj.* 西方的　　riverside〔'rɪvə,saɪd〕*n.* 河岸
try〔traɪ〕*v.* 嘗試　　hospital〔'hɑspɪtl̩〕*n.* 醫院
right〔raɪt〕*adj.* 正確的　　place〔ples〕*n.* 地方；地點
once〔wʌns〕*conj.* 一旦　　exit〔'ɛgzɪt〕*v.* 離開
station〔'steʃən〕*n.* 車站　　***turn right*** 右轉
then〔ðɛn〕*adv.* 然後　　follow〔'falo〕*adv.* 尊循
sign〔saɪn〕*n.* 標誌；牌示　　train〔tren〕*n.* 火車

20. (**A**) Question : What time is it now?
問：現在幾點？

M：My God! Look at the line. There must be a hundred
people in the line.
男：我的天呀！看看那個隊伍。一定有一百個人排隊。

W：I told you it was going to be crowded.
女：我告訴過你一定會很擠。

M：But we're an hour early! The movie starts at nine o'clock.
男：但是我們早到了一個小時！電影九點開始。

W：Is there an eleven o'clock movie? I'll bet the nine
o'clock is sold out already.
女：有十一點的場次嗎？我敢說九點的已經賣完了。

A. Eight o'clock. 八點。
B. Ten o'clock. 十點。
C. Eleven o'clock. 十一點。

* ***My God!*** 我的天呀！　　***look at*** 看　　line〔laɪn〕*n.* 隊伍
hundred〔'hʌndrəd〕*adj.* 一百的　　told〔told〕*v.* 告訴【tell 的過去式】
crowded〔'kraʊdɪd〕*adj.* 擁擠的　　hour〔aʊr〕*n.* 小時
early〔'ɝlɪ〕*adv.* (比預定時間) 早　　o'clock〔ə'klɑk〕*n.* …點鐘
bet〔bɛt〕*v.* 打賭；確定　　***I bet*** 我打賭；我敢說
be sold out 賣完

TEST 12 詳解

聽力：是非題

1. (**Y**) They are learning the alphabet.

他們正在學字母。

＊ learn〔lɜn〕v. 學習　　alphabet〔'ælfə,bɛt〕n. 字母

2. (**Y**) They are fishing.

他們正在釣魚。

＊ fish〔fɪʃ〕v. 釣魚

3. (**Y**) It is 3:15.

現在是三點十五分。

4. (**N**) There is a woman sitting at the desk.

書桌前坐著一位女士。

* ***there + be*** 有～　　sit〔sɪt〕*v.* 坐

　 desk〔dɛsk〕*n.* 書桌

5. (**Y**) The dog is very happy.

狗很高興。

* dog〔dɔg〕*n.* 狗　　happy〔'hæpɪ〕*adj.* 高興的

6. (**N**) The girls are ice-skating.

女孩們正在溜冰。

* ice-skate〔'aɪs,sket〕*v.* 溜冰

7. (**Y**) The man is cutting a cake.

男士正在切蛋糕。

* cut〔kʌt〕v. 切　　cake〔kek〕n. 蛋糕

8. (**N**) Mary is cold.

瑪麗覺得很冷。

* cold〔kold〕adj. 冷的

9. (**N**) Roger likes playing badminton.

羅傑喜歡打羽毛球。

* Roger〔'rɑdʒɚ〕*n.* 羅傑
badminton〔'bædmɪntən〕*n.* 羽毛球（運動）

10. (**Y**) This is a candy bar.

這是一條巧克力。

* candy〔'kændɪ〕*n.* 糖果   bar〔bɑr〕*n.* 棒；棒狀物
candy bar 巧克力條

聽力：選擇題

11. (**B**) Question : What did the boy do with his dishes?

問：男孩怎麼樣處置他的待洗餐具？

W : Ken, please put your dishes in the sink when you've finished eating.

女：肯，當你吃完後，請把你的待洗餐具放在水槽裡。

M : I did, Mom. I even washed the fork and spoon, like you told me.

男：我放了，媽。我甚至把叉子跟湯匙洗好了，像妳告訴過我的。

W : Hmm, then who left this bowl on the table?

女：嗯，那麼是誰把這個碗留在桌上？

M : It must have been Lisa. I didn't use a bowl. I used a plate.

男：一定是麗莎。我沒有用碗。我用盤子。

A. He used a bowl. 他用了一個碗。

B. He put them in the sink. <u>他把它們放到水槽裡。</u>

C. He didn't have any dishes. 他沒有任何的待洗餐具。

* dishes〔ˋdɪʃɪz〕*n. pl.* 待洗餐具　　Ken〔kɛn〕*n.* 肯
sink〔sɪŋk〕*n.* 水槽　　finish〔ˋfɪnɪʃ〕*v.* 完成
even〔ˋivən〕*adv.* 甚至　　wash〔wɑʃ〕*v.* 清洗
fork〔fɔrk〕*n.* 叉子　　spoon〔spun〕*n.* 湯匙
like〔laɪk〕*conj.* 像…一樣；如同
told〔told〕*v.* 告訴；吩咐【tell 的過去式】
hmm〔hm〕*interj.*（表示遲疑、停頓）唔；嗯　　then〔ðɛn〕*adv.* 那麼
left〔lɛft〕*v.* 遺留【leave 的過去式】　　bowl〔bol〕*n.* 碗
table〔ˋtebḷ〕*n.* 桌子　　***must have + p.p.*** 當時一定
Lisa〔ˋlisə〕*n.* 麗莎　　use〔juz〕*v.* 使用　　plate〔plet〕*n.* 盤子

12. (**B**) Question : What time is it now?

問：現在幾點？

M : When is the next train for Keelong?

男：下一班到基隆的火車是何時？

W : The next train leaves at five o'clock.

女：下一班火車五點開。

M : OK, good. That gives me twenty minutes to buy something to eat.

男：好的。那就給了我二十分鐘買點東西吃。

W : Don't be late. You don't want to miss the train.

女：別遲到了。你不會想要錯過這班火車。

A. 4:00. 四點。

B. 4:40. 四點四十分。

C. 5:00. 五點。

* next〔nɛkst〕*adj.* 下一個的　　train〔tren〕*n.* 火車
leave〔liv〕*v.* 離開　　o'clock〔ə'klɑk〕*n.* …點鐘
minute〔'mɪnɪt〕*n.* 分鐘　　something〔'sʌmθɪŋ〕*n.* 某物
late〔let〕*adj.* 遲到的　　miss〔mɪs〕*v.* 錯過
What time is it now? 現在幾點？

13.(**A**) Question : How much does delivery cost?

問：運費要多少錢？

W : How much does delivery cost?

女：運費要多少錢？

M : Delivery is free, but it costs 500 dollars for the workers to set up your new air conditioner .

男：免運費，但是工人裝設你的新冷氣的費用是五百元。

W : What if I do it myself?

女：如果我自己裝的話呢？

M : Then there's no extra cost.

男：那麼就沒有額外的費用。

A. Nothing. 不用錢。

B. 500 dollars. 五百元。

C. There is no delivery service. 沒有遞送服務。

* ***How much…?*** …要多少錢？　　delivery〔dɪ'lɪvərɪ〕*n.* 遞送
cost〔kɔst〕*v.* 花費　*n.* 費用　　free〔fri〕*adj.* 免費的

worker〔'wɜkɚ〕*n.* 工人　　***set up*** 裝設；安裝
new〔nu〕*adj.* 新的　　air conditioner〔ɛr kən'dɪʃənɚ〕*n.* 冷氣
What if…? 如果…的話？　　extra〔'ɛkstrə〕*adj.* 額外的
nothing〔'nʌθɪŋ〕*pron.* （什麼也）沒有　　service〔'sɜvɪs〕*n.* 服務

14. (**C**) Question : What does the man want?

問：男士想要什麼？

M : Do you have this shirt in a medium?

男：妳們的這件襯衫有中號嗎？

W : Let me check. What color do you want?

女：讓我查看看。你想要什麼顏色？

M : Green, if possible. Blue is OK, too. Anything but red.

男：綠色，如果可能的話。藍色也可以。絕對不要紅色。

W : OK. I'll be back in a minute.

女：好的。我很快就回來。

A. A small sweater in blue. 一件小號的藍色毛衣。

B. A large jacket in red. 一件大號的紅色夾克。

C. A green shirt or a blue shirt. <u>一件綠色或藍色的襯衫。</u>

* want〔wɑnt〕*v.* 想要　　shirt〔ʃɜt〕*n.* 襯衫
medium〔'midɪəm〕*n.* 中號　　check〔tʃɛk〕*v.* 檢查；查看
color〔'kʌlɚ〕*n.* 顏色　　green〔grin〕*n.* 綠色
if possible 如果可能的話　　***anything but*** 絕不
in a minute 馬上；很快（= *very soon*）
small〔smɔl〕*adj.* 小的　　sweater〔'swɛtɚ〕*n.* 毛衣
large〔lɑrdʒ〕*adj.* 大的　　jacket〔'dʒækɪt〕*n.* 夾克

15. (**B**) Question : Is Mr. Collins in the office?

問：柯林斯先生在辦公室嗎？

W : Have you seen Mr. Collins?

女：你有看到柯林斯先生嗎？

M : He's out of the office today. Why?

男：他今天不在辦公室。為什麼這麼問？

W : I have a message for him from Ms. Smith.

女：我有一個留言要給他，來自史密斯女士。

M：Leave it on his desk. He'll see it tomorrow morning.

男：放在他的辦公桌上吧。他明天早上會看到。

A. Yes, he's at his desk. 是的，他在上班。

B. No, he's not in the office. <u>不，他不在辦公室。</u>

C. No, but he left a message. 不，但他有留言。

* Collins〔'kɑlɪnz〕*n.* 柯林斯　　office〔'ɔfɪs〕*n.* 辦公室
  out of 離開　　message〔'mɛsɪdʒ〕*n.* 訊息；留言
  Smith〔smɪθ〕*n.* 史密斯　　leave〔liv〕*v.* 留；放下
  at one's ***desk*** 在上班　　***leave a message*** 留言

16. (**A**) Question : What happened to the woman?

　　　問：女士發生什麼事？

　　M：What happened to your arm?

　　男：妳的手臂怎麼了？

　　W：I fell off my bicycle yesterday.

　　女：我昨天從腳踏車上摔下來。

　　M：You need to be more careful! Is it broken?

　　男：妳必須更小心一點！有骨折嗎？

　　W：No, it's not.

　　女：不，沒有。

　　A. She fell off her bike. <u>她從腳踏車上摔下來。</u>

　　B. She fell off a ladder. 她從梯子上摔下來。

　　C. She fell down the stairs. 她從樓梯上摔下來。

　　* happen〔'hæpən〕*v.* 發生 *< to >*　　arm〔ɑrm〕*n.* 手臂
　　　fell〔fɛl〕*v.* 掉落【fall 的過去式】
　　　fall off 從…跌落　　bicycle〔'baɪsɪkl̩〕*n.* 腳踏車
　　　careful〔'kɛrfəl〕*adj.* 小心的　　broken〔'brokən〕*adj.* 骨折的
　　　bike〔baɪk〕*n.* 腳踏車　　ladder〔'lædɚ〕*n.* 梯子
　　　fall down 從…摔落　　stairs〔stɛrz〕*n. pl.* 樓梯；階梯

17. (**A**) Question : Is the man afraid of heights?

　　　問：這位男士怕高嗎？

W : Have you ever been to the top of Taipei 101?

女：你去過台北 101 的頂樓嗎？

M : No, I haven't.

男：不，沒有。

W : Really? Why not?

女：真的嗎？何不去看看？

M : First of all, I'm afraid of heights. Second, it's kind of expensive. I heard it costs 500 NT dollars.

男：首先，我怕高。第二，這有點貴。我聽說這樣要花五百元新台幣。

A. Yes, he is. 是的，他怕高。

B. No, he isn't. 不，他不怕高。

C. Sometimes, he does. 有時候他會。

* **be afraid of** 害怕　　**heights** 〔 haɪts 〕 *n. pl.* 高處
  have been to 曾經去過　　top 〔 tɑp 〕 *n.* 頂端　　***Why not?*** 何不？
  first of all 首先；第一點　　second 〔'sɛkənd 〕 *adv.* 其次；第二點
  kind of 有點 (= *a little*)　　expensive 〔 ɪk'spɛnsɪv 〕 *adj.* 昂貴的
  cost 〔 kɔst 〕 *v.* (事物) 花費　　dollar 〔'dɑlɚ 〕 *n.* 元
  NT dollar 新台幣 (= *New Taiwan dollar*)
  sometimes 〔'sʌm,taɪmz 〕 *adv.* 有時候；偶爾

18. (**A**) Question : What time does the party start?

問：派對幾點開始？

M : Tomorrow is Cindy's birthday and we're having a party. Would you like to come?

男：明天是辛蒂的生日，而且我們將要舉辦一個派對。妳想要來嗎？

W : I'm sorry, I can't make it. I'm going to see a movie with my boyfriend.

女：很抱歉，我不能去。我要跟我的男朋友去看電影。

M : Well, the party starts at seven, if you change your mind.

男：嗯，派對七點開始，如果妳改變心意的話。

W : Maybe we'll stop by after the movie is over.

女：或許我們會在電影結束後順路過去看看。

A. Seven o'clock. 七點。
B. Eight o'clock. 八點。
C. When the movie ends. 當電影結束時。

* party〔'partɪ〕n. 派對　　Cindy〔'sɪndɪ〕n. 辛蒂
birthday〔'bɝθ,de〕n. 生日　　**have a party** 舉辦派對
would like to V. 想要~　　**make it** 成功；辦到；能來
see a movie 看電影　　boyfriend〔'bɔɪ,frɛnd〕n. 男朋友
well〔wɛl〕*interj.*（表示停頓、遲疑）嗯
change one's **mind** 改變心意　　maybe〔'mebɪ〕*adv.* 或許；可能
stop by 順路探望；順路拜訪　　over〔'ovɚ〕*adj.* 結束的
start〔start〕n. 開始　　end〔ɛnd〕v. 結束

19. (**C**) Question : What does the man tell the woman to do?
問：男士告訴女士要做什麼？
W : There's something wrong with my computer. All of a
sudden, it stopped working.
女；我的電腦出了問題。突然間，它就停止運作了。
M : What's the problem? Is the power on? Did you make
sure it's plugged in?
男：問題是什麼？電源有開嗎？妳確定有插電嗎？
W : Yes, I've even tried restarting, but nothing is happening.
女：有的，我甚至試過重開機，但是什麼也沒發生。
M : Then I don't know what to do. You should call a
repairman.
男：那我就不知道要做什麼了。你應該打電話給維修人員。

A. Unplug the computer. 拔掉電腦的插頭。
B. Restart the computer. 電腦重新開機。
C. Call a repairman. 打電話給維修人員。

* **there's something wrong with**… …有問題；…出了毛病
computer〔kəm'pjutɚ〕n. 電腦　　sudden〔'sʌdn〕*adj.* 突然的
all of a sudden 突然地（= *suddenly*）　　stop〔stap〕v. 停止
work〔wɝk〕v. 運作　　problem〔'prabləm〕n. 問題
power〔'pauɚ〕n. 電；電源　　on〔an〕*adj.* 開著的
make sure 確定　　plug〔plʌg〕v. 塞住　　**plug in** 將…接通電源

try〔traɪ〕 v. 嘗試　　restart〔͵rɪ'stɑrt〕 v. 重新啟動
happen〔'hæpən〕 v. 發生　　call〔kɔl〕 v. 打電話給（人）
repairman〔rɪ'pɛrmən〕 n. 維修人員
unplug〔ʌn'plʌg〕 v. 拔去⋯的插頭

20. (**C**) Question : What is the woman's score on the entrance exam?

問：女士的入學考試考得如何？

M : How did you do on the entrance exam?

男：妳入學考試考得如何？

W : It's hard to say.　We won't know until the scores are posted, will we?　I think I did pretty well.　I studied and felt like I had all the answers.　And you?

女：很難說。我們要直到分數公布才會知道，是吧？我認為我考得很好。我有讀書，而且我覺得我都會。你呢？

M : I'm not so sure.　I studied as well, but some of the material was new to me.

男：我沒那麼確定。我也有讀，但有些內容對我而言還是很陌生。

W : Oh, do you mean the questions at the end?　I wasn't prepared for those.

女：喔，你指的是最後的那些題目嗎？我沒有準備那些。

A. She did well. 她考得很好。
B. She did poorly. 她考得很差。
C. She doesn't know her score yet. <u>她還不知道她的分數。</u>

* score〔skor〕 n. 分數　　entrance〔'ɛntrəs〕 n. 進入；入學
exam〔ɪg'zæm〕 n. 考試　　do〔du〕 v. 表現
hard〔hɑrd〕 adj. 困難的　　post〔post〕 v. 發表；公告
do well 考得好　　pretty〔'prɪtɪ〕 adv. 非常
study〔'stʌdɪ〕 v. 讀書　　*feel like*⋯ 覺得好像⋯
have all the answers 什麼都知道；無所不知（= *know all the answers*）
sure〔ʃur〕 adj. 確定的　　*as well* 也（= *too*）
material〔mə'tɪrɪəl〕 n. 資料　　new〔nju〕 adj. 新的；陌生的
mean〔min〕 v. 意思是　　prepared〔prɪ'pɛrd〕 adj. 有準備的
poorly〔'purlɪ〕 adv. 差勁地　　*not⋯yet* 尚未

編者的話

親愛的讀者：

　　現在學英文非常簡單，用「手機」就可以學了。我50多年教學的精華，都會在「快手」中播放，歡迎大家模仿我。在課堂上，教我「快手」上的作品，馬上變成名師，學生會愈來愈多，也歡迎在線上模仿我，期待青出於藍而勝於藍！用我研發的教材，最安全，經過層層的校對。一定要學從美國人嘴巴裡說出來的話，且自己每天也能脫口而出。

　　學會話的方法是：一口氣說出三句話，我們要背就背最好的，例如：「由你決定。」最好的三句英文是：You're the boss. 字面的意思是「你是老闆。」You call the shots.（你發號施令，我開槍射擊。）Your wish is my command.（你的希望就是你給我的命令。）當你一口氣說這三句幽默的話，任何人都會佩服你。我花費了好幾年的功夫，才把這三句話累積在一起，人人愛聽！

　　英文不使用，就會忘記！「使用、使用、再使用」，教自己「背過」、「使用過的」句子，有靈魂、有魅力，是上網教學的最高境界！網路上，有網路紅人亂造句子，亂說一通，太可怕了！期待他盡快撤下來。人最怕「吃錯藥」、「學錯東西」。

「英文順口溜」一口氣說三句，特別好聽

　　「快手」和「抖音」是大陸的兩個大平台，有80多萬中外英文老師在發表作品，我每天上午和下午各發表一次。如果「作品」不被人接受，馬上就會被淘汰。

　　以前，我從來沒有想到，會有這個機會，把我50多年來上課的精華，在手機上發表。過去大家用文法自行造句、自行寫文章，太可怕了！我們問過100多位英文老師：「這裡是哪裡？」大家都翻成：Where is here? (誤) 應該是：Where am I? 或 Where are we? 才對。同樣地，「我喜歡這裡。」不能說成 I like here. (誤) 要說：I like it here. 才正確。這種例子不勝枚舉！結論：背極短句最安全。

　　我們發明「英文順口溜」，一口氣說三句，創造了優美的語言，說出來特別好聽。說一句話沒有感情，一口氣說：I like it here. I love it here. This is my kind of place. (我喜歡這裡。我愛這裡。這是我喜歡的地方。) 三句話綁在一起，隨口就可說出，多麼令人感到溫暖啊！

　　今天鍾藏政董事長傳來好消息，我在「抖音」上的粉絲已經超過20萬人了。感謝「小芝」充當攝影師，感謝「北京101名師工廠」讓我一輩子的心血，能夠發光發亮，「劉毅英文」全體的努力當然功不可沒。我們一定要持續努力，來感謝大家的支持。

讓我們幫助你成為說英文高手

「英文順口溜」即將出版！一切以「記憶」和「實用性」為最優先。以三句為一組，一開口，就是三句話，說出來非常熱情，有溫度。

例如：你已經會說："Thank you." 「英文順口溜」教你："Thank you. I appreciate it. I owe you."（謝謝你。我很感謝。我虧欠你。）我們不只在學英文，還在學「口才」，每天說好聽的話，人見人愛。

又如："It's my treat. It's on me. Let me pay."（我請客。我請客。讓我來付錢。）學英文不忘發揚中國人好客的文化。一般人道歉時，只會說："I'm sorry." 背了「英文順口溜」，你會說："I'm sorry. I apologize. It's my fault."（對不起。我道歉。是我的錯。）先從三句開始，會愈說愈多，你還可以加上三句："I was wrong. You are right. Please forgive me."（我錯了。你是對的。請原諒我。）

「英文順口溜」先在「快手」和「抖音」上教，大家可以在「手機」上免費學。我受益很多，期待分享給所有人！

掃描下載快手APP

下載「快手」及「抖音」，免費學「英文順口溜」

　　原來，「說一口流利的英語」是最漂亮的衣服、成功的象徵（a sign of success），苦練出來的英文最美。（The most beautiful English is learned through hard work.）

　　現在，用我們新發明的「英文順口溜」，靠手機APP「快手」就可以輕鬆背好，一口氣說出來，很有信心。例如，一般美國人再見時多說："Bye!" 我們會說："See you soon. See you around. Have a good one."（待會見。回頭見。祝你有美好的一天。）中文要改變語言不容易，但是利用學英文的機會訓練口才，變成體貼、熱情、感恩的人，只要背我們研發的「英文順口溜」，一定可以做到！

　　說話是一種藝術，需要認真學習，說話代表你的「修養、教育、人品」。叫別人不要遲到，不要說："Don't be late. Don't make me wait."（不要遲到。不要讓我等。）可以說：I'll be there on time. On the dot. On the nose.（我會準時到。會準時。非常準時。）成功的人，說話更要客氣、有禮貌，不能讓你身邊的人有壓力。

劉毅